MW01243873

How   To   Develop

A
GOAL
MIND

How To Develop

A GOAL MIND

*Using Left and Right Brain Functions
to Achieve Your Goals*

ERMA ROQUEMORE

Published by
CONTRAST PUBLISHING©
Tulsa, Oklahoma

First Edition Copyright© 1993
by Erma J. Roquemore
Revised Second Edition Copyright© 1995
All rights reserved
Manufactured in the USA

Cover Design: Stephanie M. Lesko
Interior Design: Egret Design
Editing: Andrea Tronslin

Library of Congress Catalog Number: 93-92635
ISBN 1-882518-19-9

To Jason, Gina, and Joel

ACKNOWLEDGMENTS

As I worked through the completion of this edition, I relocated to Tulsa, Oklahoma. There was, no doubt, a bittersweet emotion involved with leaving friends and family. Prior to making the decision, I contacted several individuals who worked closely with me on this edition. Although they shared my sentiments surrounding the move, they promised to keep in touch and assist me in any and every way possible. It is difficult to find words to express how they have touched me, with numerous phone calls, voice messages and letters, asking that I obtain certain issues of magazines, books and talk show transcripts in support of this edition. It truly attests to the fact that they all *undeniably* and *genuinely* support my efforts. Mucho thanks to all of you. Thanks to my mother, Pearline, whose consistent, reliable and right-on feedback provided a source of motivation and humor. Mom, if you have not purchased stock in your long-distance carrier, you should. Brenda Lloyd-Jones, Ph.D., has been extremely instrumental in my integration to Tulsa. I thank you for all the invitations to the many formal, and sometimes not so formal, political and community functions. Your discerning ear and lucid feedback are invaluable and very much appreciated. To the entire staff of Egret Design, thanks a bunch for your lengthy discussions regarding the exterior and interior design of the book. You provided a lot of handholding during this process. Thanks for your diplomacy and sensitivity in areas that were unknown to me. All of you have been quite generous in the allocation of your time and technical expertise. Many thanks to Peggy Striegel of Striegel & Associates, for graciously providing continuity between media contacts I had in Southern California and now in Tulsa. Thanks for your sincerity and thoughtfulness, Peggy.

Above *all*, I thank God and give Him the glory. During this transition, I have depended solely on Him to provide direction, wisdom and serenity. I thank Him for providing hindsight, foresight and insight throughout all my endeavors and will continue to submit myself to Him as an open vessel, so He can perform great works through me.

TABLE OF CONTENTS

PREFACE

In the fall of 1981, I took a close look at myself in an attempt to identify aspects of my personality and character that prevented me from being a success. I sincerely felt I was doing all the right things. I thought about, talked about, and dreamed about my goals.

It was only after talking, one evening, to my younger sister about the logistics of goal setting that I realized what I had been doing wrong. For years, I only thought about the things I wanted to do. I had never taken the time to commit my thoughts to paper.

The very next day during lunch, I sat down and listed every goal I wanted to accomplish over the next three months. The list also included anything I felt would help or hinder me. For the first time, I was really excited about the prospect of accomplishing my goals. Later, I stopped by my sister's house and followed her from room to room, ardently sharing each goal with her. For the first time, I felt I was on the right track and knew exactly what I needed to do in order to accomplish my goals. There is a strange and uplifting feeling you get when you have a revelation about something. You want to shout it from the rooftops and let everyone know. Yet, if you are like me, you are compelled to simply work through that vision silently, putting its velocity and veracity to the test. That is what I did.

For the next three months, I managed to avoid everyone and everything that would prevent me from achieving my goals. Initially, you may find this to be one of the most difficult things to do. For me, it was emotionally taxing to tell people I was not available after work or that I was busy when they phoned, after being so accessible in the past. However, at the end of three months, all but one goal was achieved, and that was to purchase a book on how to maintain saltwater fish. Earlier that year, I had contemplated purchasing an aquarium.

That was over a decade ago. Today, I realize that I have additional faculties I can tap in order to enhance my goaltending techniques. I discovered that by exercising left and right brain functions, I could augment my current regimen and obtain additional insight into the potential power within me.

There are two distinct sides of the brain. Each side has physical and intellectual boundaries, in terms of how various aspects of our behavior, judgment and emotions are governed. Over the last two decades, there has been an enormous amount of research conducted on the disparities between male and female brains. This research has shown that men and women access different parts of their brains to accomplish the same task. We also have a tendency to rely more on one side over the other. In other words, although we are left- and right-brained, we typically neglect one side and have more of a comfort level with using the other to problem solve and for information processing. Realizing that left brain individuals process and perceive situations differently from right brain folks led me to a greater awareness of my own capabilities.

From the moment of my discovery, I began to examine various ways in which I approached problem solving. In addition, I identified what I believed to be my natural talents. Interestingly, the characteristics I regarded as inherent leaned towards both left and right brain operations. I enjoy creative problem solving as much as I welcome a logical step-by-step approach to working through issues.

Over the years, documenting my goals has become somewhat of a ritual with me. My goals are in full view of anyone entering my home. There is a large placard that lists all my goals by category. It is standard practice for me to set spiritual, financial, personal, physical and business goals. As one goal is completed, another takes its place. I also document critical success factors, affirmations and those things that will help or hinder me.

The techniques I employ are contained throughout the pages of this book. These methods will provide you with a proven formula for realizing and accomplishing your goals. They guide you through self-directed exercises designed to provide a framework for determining right or left brain propensity, and assist you with planning for success in all aspects of your life. The visualization techniques are intended to help you develop or strengthen yourself in this area. As you employ self-visualization strategies, you will begin to preview your success. This will help keep you motivated and on track. Additionally, as you read the segment on male and female brain patterns, my objective is to have you walk away with an elevated understanding of the contrast between genders and a greater appreciation of the differences. So get some paper and a pencil, find a comfortable chair, keep your mind open and get ready to direct your path to success.

Erma Roquemore

PART I

CHAPTER ONE

PURPOSE OF
SETTING GOALS

... [Purpose] acquires meaning as part of an ongoing process; its certification lies, not in rhetoric, but in performance.

—Arthur M. Schlesinger, Jr.

There are many reasons why we set goals. Some individuals set goals for personal reasons, others for the psychological perks they receive by challenging and stretching themselves. People with clear, well-thought-out goals know where they are going, how they are going to get there and how long it will take them. These folks lead happy, productive and successful lives. They all share a common blueprint for successful living, and that is to have a purpose, an aim and a target. They also know that if you don't stand for something, you will fall for anything.

Establishing a goal is more difficult than accomplishing one, because it requires knowing your strengths and weaknesses. Ask anyone who is struggling with the prospect of goal-setting what their individual challenges are and they will probably tell you they do not *really* know. They may acknowledge having a variety of things they are good at and would like to venture into. However, they will readily attest to the fact that they have a tough time identifying and harnessing their skills and talents. So, we need to set goals to help keep us motivated, on track and feeling good about ourselves. How do you know if you have arrived at your destination if you never mapped it out?

Start With A Clean Slate

In order to have a point of reference, you will need to start with a clean slate. Doing this will require you to toss out outmoded thoughts and methods. In another segment, I will go into more detail about the steps necessary to document and accomplish your goals. But you must begin by clearing the cobwebs from any previous attempts and leave yourself open to see your way. Do not become frustrated with the process, because it is not easy to define and document your goals. The reason you may have some difficulty getting started is that most people only think about the things they want to do; they do not write them down. Thinking about something is very easy to do, especially considering the brain uses only about 10 watts of electricity. You begin to realize that entertaining passive thoughts is really a no-brainer. Even if you get thoroughly excited about the notion and wax enthusiastic, you still would not generate the motivation, need or energy required to put those thoughts on paper.

You must commit these thoughts to paper, and come to terms with all aspects of completing each task. For some, this may create anxieties that turn to fear. If you dwell on them too long, the fear turns to lack of activity and thoughts of "Oh, I can't do this, I don't know why I ever thought I could." Several weeks or months later, those thoughts (which, some believed to be goals) have no more substance, weight or velocity than they did when first envisioned.

Learn From Other's Mistakes

You could talk to hundreds of people about goal setting and ask them point blank, "Do you have any goals?" The overwhelming majority will immediately improve their posture and reply "Of course I have goals, doesn't everybody?" However, if you were to ask them what the goals are and what steps they are planning to accomplish them, many would begin to stammer, pause, and quickly look away from you and say, "Well, I haven't thought about all of the steps involved, but I know pretty much what I need to do." The simple truth is, most people do not know where they are going or how they are going to get there because they have not taken the time to C.H.A.R.T.© a course for themselves, which I will explain in a later segment. It may sound simple, but it's true: a goal and a thought are not synonymous. When you think about things you want to do, all you are doing is thinking about them. It is nothing more than an idea, a thought—and a fleeting thought, at best. Only 3 percent of the population documents their goals. Another 10 percent just think about them and the other 87 percent just casually drift through each day without any aim or direction. Until you take the time to commit your thoughts to paper, they are nothing more than thoughts.

Lillian Hellman said that "... It is considered unhealthy in America to remember mistakes, neurotic to think about them, psychotic to dwell on them." However, we can all learn from other people's mistakes and try very hard not to make the same ones. Psychologists say we can learn a lot by watching daytime talk shows. Although these shows are labeled trash television, we can work through our own personal issues by listening to other folks discuss theirs. You do not have to reinvent the wheel and duplicate your efforts. Just listen, watch and talk to others who are successfully doing the things that interest you. It is also stimulating to talk with successful people, because they will usually engage you and talk about what it took for them to get where they are in life. There is not one instance where I can recall having asked someone how they identified and managed their success and have that person tell me, "It's none of your business" or, "I'd rather not share the secrets of my success." Successful people love to tell others how and what to do in order to become a success. On their way up the ladder of success, they asked others and were equally engaged. Sometimes it takes us many years to understand our purpose in life. Once you grasp life's meaning, understand your position in it and all the incredible things you can accomplish, the purpose of goal setting becomes more lucid.

The Road To Success Is Strewn With...

If you know where you are going, you will get there. If you take the time to identify and document your goals, the road may be filled with challenges, but you will be better prepared to handle them. If your destination is undefined and you are hazy about your future, you will go through life aimlessly without a target or goal. Without mapping out a written course, you will live life as a victim, accepting situations and challenges without having a framework in place to support or sustain you. Do not be fooled into thinking that successful people got to where they are by talking about what they wanted to do. It has been said that the road to success is strewn with good intentions. You can say you are sincere about what you want out of life, but without documenting your goals and setting a direction, you are sincerely wrong. So, the purpose of goal setting is to provide some direction in your life. Goals keep you going and growing. They help you stay focused, disciplined and organized. They present opportunities and challenges. The opportunity is in identifying and defining the goals; the challenge is in achieving them. Every astronaut, sea captain and pilot knows his or her destination, even though the destination cannot be seen for well over 90 percent of the voyage.

But each of them set a path, knew the beginning, middle and ending positions and how long it would take them to reach their destinations. Notwithstanding any unforeseen conditions, they all reached their mark.

Recently, I was at the local library, waiting in line to check out some books. In front of me was a teenager who wanted to renew a couple of books he had returned late, but still needed to complete a book report. The woman assisting him asked how much longer he would need the books and his reply was, "I don't know." She asked him whether or not he had started writing his book report and he replied, "No, I haven't started yet." Then she asked him, "When is the book report due?" and he said, "This Friday." She smiled and said, "Well, you probably need to start sometime soon, wouldn't you say?" He shrugged his shoulder and said, "Well, I guess so." This teenager had what appeared to be good intentions. He checked the books out twice, yet had not started his book report. Although he was sincere about doing the report and probably had every intention of completing it, he was sincerely wrong in his approach. It was evident from that brief dialogue between them that he had not set a goal for meeting his obligation.

Where are you going? Do you know how you will get there? How long will it take? What do you need to help you along the way? If you cannot answer these questions with any conviction, you will have difficulty reaching your destination because you do not know what or where it is. People without clearly defined goals are like ships without rudders. They float haphazardly through life fidgeting, fumbling and fooling around. Many of them have good intentions and just do not know how to get started. Until you establish clear, concise goals, you will never recognize or stretch the potential within you.

GOALS VS. OBJECTIVES

The way to success: first have a clear goal, not a fuzzy one...

—Norman Vincent Peale

Goals and objectives are not synonymous. Although many people like to use the two terms interchangeably, they are in fact different. In terms of how they fit into the scheme of goal setting, it is important to understand that a goal states what you plan to do and an objective states how and when you will do it. At one time, a goal for my nephew was to own a CD player. He established an objective to set aside up to 30 percent more of his weekly allowance and purchase it by the first of June. I worked with him to ensure the goal would be met by helping him document it. When the two of us got together, he explained what it was he wanted to accomplish. After we talked about the various types of CD players on the market and the broad price ranges, he had an idea of what he would need to save in a few months to purchase the one he wanted. What I recommended that he do was document his goal and put it someplace he frequented on a daily basis, so he could keep it in front of him. We sat down and documented it in this manner:

Goal

Statement: I want to purchase a $79.00 CD player.

Objectives: Price various models
- ☐ Determine how much more I need to save weekly
- ☐ Begin saving 4/1/95
- ☐ Purchase by June 1

This goal is pretty straightforward and to the point. It is clear what he wants to do and how and when he plans to do it. If at any time he changes his goal statement, he can alter the objectives to make certain they are in alignment with his new goal statement. After months of saving, my nephew accomplished his goal. When I talked to him at length about it, he was quite honest and told me how he got off the track a few times and what caused him to deviate from his plan. Although he completed his goal three weeks later than his original target date, he did what he set out to do. He also learned from his miscalculations and errors. What he lacked in clarity in redefining his objectives, he gained in discovering how to make adjustments and triumph over odds. He is sixteen years old and well on his way to a successful and thriving lifestyle.

Take A Strategic Look At Your Goals

Goals and objectives can also be viewed as strategies and tactics respectively. Let us gain more insight into what that means. Take into consideration the meaning of the words *strategy* and *tactic*. Both refer to a well-thought-out plan intended to put someone or something in an advantageous position prior to actual engagement with the target. A closer look at the two reveals their potential for success when utilized properly as part of the goal setting process. A strategy is a definite plan or goal you implement. A tactic goes further by defining the methods you will use in order to work through your objectives. In other words, a tactic usually develops from a strategy and defines the manner in which the goal is realized.

Be Prepared For Change

Remember, your goals and objectives may change due to a variety of things that may be out of your control. A very dear friend of mine is accustomed to documenting her goals. We talk a great deal about the positive effects this process has on our individual success. I had an opportunity to talk with her recently about a plan she developed to expand her child care service. She looked at several options in her area and decided on increasing the hours of service and adding a second center in an upscale neighborhood. She was quite excited about the second location because the area had a large number of restaurants and movie theaters. Her plan also included raising her hourly rate and accepting up to three times more children than previously.

Unfortunately, the state laws changed and she had to revamp her plan. The state required her to make changes in the hot food program she offered. She had to quickly spin on a dime, so to speak, and look into the cost of having the ceiling raised and obtaining a commercial refrigerator. Otherwise, she would have to make arrangements with the local McDonald's and pizza chains to accommodate her hot food program. Despite changes to her objectives, her original goal remained intact. You will run into a variety of obstacles that will affect your plan. As a matter of fact, they will seek you out like a magnet. If your goals are documented and you have your objectives outlined, these changes will prove more bearable. Imagine setting a goal to change your diet to that of a vegetarian. You may find going to the health food store and spending up to 30 percent more on your grocery bill not in sync with your financial goals to save an additional 12 percent of your income. In order to meet both goals, you may make some adjustments in your objectives. This could mean changing your diet to gradually introduce these foods as part of your daily consumption. Perhaps you may decide that over a period of one year you will make a complete 180 degree turnaround in your general dietary intake. This would be reasonable and also realistic, considering it takes many years to develop our taste buds for specific foods. There is also a tendency to get into fast and processed foods which makes the transition to a healthy regimen more challenging. You need to understand that *any* change, no matter how small or large, is a step in the right direction.

By gradually changing your diet, you accomplish several things. First, you give yourself a chance to see just how the change is going to impact your eating and purchasing habits. You may find yourself eating more, eating less or just trying a lot of new foods for which you haven't acquired a taste. Moreover, you allow yourself time to experiment with new recipes. This will help heighten your interest and keep you motivated to continue. Remember, changing your diet takes a lot of control, effort and determination.

Finally, you give your body a chance to adjust to newfound constraints on its digestive system. This may take some getting used to. Nonetheless, the overall results are infectious, in terms of how they permeate your entire being. They help reshape your thoughts, strengthen your mental and emotional powers, and increase your capacity to achieve the highest level of success.

So when establishing goals, make certain you keep them separate from, but aligned with your objectives. You may totally abandon a goal if you feel it is not realistic or your interests have changed. We all encounter changes in our lives that require us to make adjustments. Many of us have had to streamline a goal to keep it manageable and attainable. The intent is to make certain the goal is designed not only to keep you focused and motivated but also to afford you an opportunity to make the most of your talents.

ARE GOALS NECESSARY
FOR SUCCESS

What is known as success assumes nearly as many aliases as there are those who seek it.

—Stephen Birmingham

ottie Walters, world famous speaker says "A goal is a dream with a deadline." For me, a goal takes on several forms. First, the definition of a goal states what is to be done. Secondly, the development of a goal outlines its logical design. Finally, the achievement of a goal describes its successful execution. But just proclaiming this is not enough. You will need to take your thoughts from a subconscious level and raise them to a higher position that is more directed and focused. By doing this we elevate our goals to a conscious level and provide a basis for dealing with them sensibly.

What does it mean to raise your base-level goals to a higher level? It refers to utilizing all your faculties in order to establish and accomplish a task. But, how and where do you begin to enlist the assistance of your inherent skills? Prior to getting started, you will benefit greatly by gaining a better understanding of how you generally approach and solve various problems. First, you need to answer the question of whether or not goals are necessary. If there is anything in life you aspire to, you must have established, well-documented goals in order to attain it. So, in that respect, goals are absolutely necessary. Once you acknowledge the need, it is easier to begin defining the steps necessary to work towards the realization of your goals.

In 1981, if you asked me if I were doing all the right things to accomplish my goals, I would have said yes. I was thinking, dreaming, talking and sharing my dreams. I misled myself to believe that by exercising these emotions, I could force them to fruition. Now I realize that nothing good ever comes from force. Good things come smoothly, easily and gently. I also felt that because I was talking about my goals, they would come that much faster. I have learned, however, you do not have to talk about them, because when you are busy working towards your goals, you do not have the time.

You Could Be Your Own Worst Enemy

A gentleman who attended a couple of workshops I conducted told me he had his mind made up to own a house, run his own business, get married someday and start a family. In April of 1994, I saw him at a concert and we talked briefly about how his plan was progressing. He hesitantly told me he had not made much progress and he just needed to meditate more on what he wanted to do. He felt he just "wasn't giving it enough thought." I asked him if he had documented what he wanted to do and he replied, "I just don't seem to have the time, since I've taken on this new job." I gave him that look that said, "Sure. Yeah. Right."

We went our separate ways, but I thought about him later and really wished I could have done more to help him, right at that precise moment. Perhaps I did help, but I am not certain to what extent. He presents himself as an outgoing, energetic guy who knows what he wants and probably thinks a lot about those things. He just has not taken the time to redirect that energy and commit those thoughts to paper, so he can keep them in front of him and make his dreams a reality. Until he makes an effort to do this, he will more than likely find people, things and situations he believes are standing in the way of his success. Whether these conditions exist or are just part of his imagination, they will continue to keep his dreams at bay. If you find yourself in the same situation, do not be an enemy to yourself. Take the time to consider all aspects of what it is you are trying to accomplish. Review each item individually for its own merit. Take the things that do not fit out of the mix. Proceed with each item until you have a manageable, clearly defined set of goals you feel you can attain. Only then will you begin working towards your success.

Try The Ol' It May Work For You, But Not For Me

It almost seems a bit senseless to raise the question of whether or not goals are necessary because all successful people set goals for themselves. These folks are action and results oriented. Do not think for one minute they were all born that way. It is a behavior everyone learns. Goals are at the foundation of every success-based transaction. When you raise your default (subconscious) goals to conscious goals, you turn negative thinking into positive thinking.

A good friend shared a goal with me not long ago. She felt our educational system neglected science as a subject in our public schools and wanted to establish a mobile science clinic. I was impressed with the notion and asked her how she would go about developing this idea. Her responses were really dynamic and concise. It was evident she was jazzed about the idea. I was happy for her and suggested she write down what she felt was necessary to pull this off. She agreed to do this and get back with me.

About two weeks later, I had an opportunity to see her and her son at church and asked her what progress had been made on her new venture. Sadly, she had not done one thing that would help bring her dream closer to reality. She remarked "Oh Erma, you're the one who's good at doing all the documenting and writing here and there. That stuff works for you, but not for me. I'm just going to have to make some contacts, go right to the source and see if I can get funding." What she failed to realize is that in order to obtain funding, she will need to put her thoughts on paper and present them in some logical, concise format. If she is attempting to sell a banker on her ideas, she will need a business plan. Which, in effect, will define her goals in significant detail.

Excuses, Excuses, Excuses

In the previous example, as in others, there has been one constant; everyone pointed to some person, place or thing that stood in the way of their success. In other words, they had excuses, not reasons for missing the mark. There is a distinction between the two. More often than not, we have a tendency to make excuses for our inability to fulfill a promise. First, let me define the composition of an excuse and a reason. A reason justifies why you were unable to follow through on a promise, act or deed. It provides logic and a basis for such. When you state a reason that something was not done, you substantiate the sense behind it and leave room to state how and when you will complete it. An excuse begs for some sort of pardon or forgiveness. It states rather weakly why you did not follow through; it has less significance and veracity than a reason. When a person presents an excuse for not providing something, they are asking to be relieved and even exempt from the responsibility of fulfilling it.

This is an extremely important factor when determining whether or not goals are really necessary. If you do not create goals for yourself, it's much easier to make excuses when you are not successful in personal and professional ventures. Imagine this scenario:

A parent, having noticed his child's grades slipping, promises to spend more time assisting him with his homework and providing guidance. Several months go by and the child brings another progress report home, exhibiting lower grades in two classes. After reviewing the report, the parent begins to question the child, asking why he did not remind him and asking why the child cannot do better.

This scenario is commonplace. We say we are going to do something and when we don't complete the task, we search for excuses. When we have an opportunity to demonstrate our ineptness, we are often quick to put the blame on someone or something else. If you really give it some thought, you will realize that in order to make a cogent excuse, you have to dig for it. Such excuses do not come easily because, by definition, we need to find a circumstance, person or thing that somehow fits the flimsy framework of the story. Usually, the excuse is weak, which is evident by the facial expression of the person on the receiving end of the tale.

So, whenever people raise the question of whether or not goals are necessary, ask yourself this question: *Are they looking for an excuse to avoid success?* If you have to question it, you may not be ready for the challenge. Instead, you may be trying to hide behind a cloak of indecisiveness and excuses. The longer you put off getting started, the more comfortable you become with your ability to find excuses. A couple who does not set financial goals exists from paycheck to paycheck, spending money without regard to the overall impact it may have on their future. Parents who don't initiate goals to spend more time with their kids position themselves and their children for failure. People who go through life without charting a course are planning to flounder. My response to whether or not goals are necessary is a resounding yes. You must have a dream if you are going to make a dream come true. And, in order to achieve success, you must establish goals. They should be clearly planned and documented in order to satisfy your thirst for success and help direct your path to affluence and prosperity.

CHAPTER FOUR

HOW ATTITUDE
AFFECTS GOALS

*It is better to be
looked over
than
overlooked.*

—Mae West

I once read that attitude is more important than aptitude. It is true that your attitude will determine your altitude in life. In other words, the ladder of success has many rungs with no predetermined number. It is up to you to determine that number because you design it. You are the architect of *your* ladder of success. Have no qualms about it; that ladder is not crowded at the top, but it is jam-packed at the bottom. Your attitude will be a major factor in deciding how high the ladder will be and the number of rungs it will have. Some folks think they can skip some steps on the way up, but they are deceiving themselves. You cannot take short cuts in life and expect to sustain any true level of success.

Prepare And Be Optimistic

When you prepare yourself for success, part of the process involves having an open mind and a fresh attitude. Any preconceived notions about how things are going to work out, who you will encounter, and how you will behave should be eliminated. You must start with a clean slate and perish any thoughts that may prevent you from embracing the light, so to speak. Individuals with a zest for life view as a challenge what most people consider a problem. They wake up each day giving thanks for being alive and knowing that this is the first day of the rest of their lives. They know you must live each day as though it is your last. My parents, from whom I get so much of my motivation and drive, used to say, "Erma, your days are numbered. You don't know how long you're going to be on this earth. So, you better make the most of every day." When I was growing up, I heard that quite a bit and my brother considered it a "stock statement." We did not have much in terms of money, fancy things, vacations or nice clothes. However, my parents imparted strong values to us and always told us our attitude would either make us or break us. Throughout life, we hear and often read these kinds of statements and sometimes they affect us immediately. Other times, we are not directly impacted until we have encountered *many* situations that bear some resemblance to a particular statement; then it somehow sinks in.

Stop, Look And Listen

I conducted a seminar for a singles' ministry, and during the break, a man walked up to me and said, "You know, this may sound funny, but when you were talking, some of the things you said felt like you were talking directly to me." He went on to tell me what particular statements had affected him and although he had heard those same things most of his life, somehow they had more meaning to him. He said, "It seems as though you're saying, Roger, now this one's for you, so wake up." You can probably identify with this and have a similar situation you can recall. People close to you have told you things for *years* that make a heck of a lot of sense, and you turn a deaf ear. But let a neighbor, friend or stranger tell you and all of a sudden it makes so much sense. The reason is that, at certain times in our lives, for one reason or another we close ourselves off to accepting practical advice. Our attitude is at a level that is pretty close to cavalier. When this happens, typically one of two situations exist: We are either too young and do not have enough exposure in life to realize we *should* listen and take heed, or, we are at that age where we think we know it all. In other words, we think we are "all that" and do not have a *need* to listen. At some point, however, we come to our senses. When we do, we are sometimes sorry we did not do it sooner.

What Is Your AQ?

Your AQ, or attitudinal quotient, defines the frequency with which you transform what could be a negative situation into a positive one. With each statement you make, on any given day, you have an opportunity to raise your AQ. This is how it works: When anyone approaches you who is having a bad hair day, tell yourself you have two options; you can turn it around, or *you* can be turned around. You can accept the verbal litter being thrown in your direction or turn the situation around by recycling the trash. How do you recycle the trash? You can take the same approach you would with normal rubbish. Separate that which can be reused, or the value in what is being said, from the real garbage or pessimistic statements. Wrap the real garbage in a brief and direct response that communicates your indifference to that aspect of their statement. Finally, recycle the valuable portion, using organized, intelligent phrases that allows you to turn the situation around, thus increasing your AQ. When your mind is on success, you do not have time for verbal litterbugs. Using this tactic will help you immediately resolve any extreme and negative behavior from others. As you exercise this option on a consistent basis, it becomes effortless.

Left And Right Brain Attitudes

Zig Ziglar says "An optimist is a person who, when he wears out his shoes, just figures he's back on his feet." An optimist sees the bright side of things. To him, the glass of water is half full. The pessimist will see the same glass as half empty, because the optimist is putting water into the glass and the pessimist is taking water out of the glass. The left and right brain also differ, in terms of their attitudinal characteristics. Because of the dissimilar organization of each side, they develop significantly different personalities. For example, the right brain tends to look at things negatively and emotionally. The left brain is more positive and logical. Something as simple as having a conversation with someone is experienced differently by the left brain than the right. The left brain will respond to the literal meaning of the words it hears without much regard to inflection. Conversely, the right brain will pick up facial expressions, body language and tone of voice without much notice given to the words. The words are coming from the speaker's left brain. The tone of voice, facial expressions and body language are coming from his right brain. So, once again we see that both sides of the brain work simultaneously to perform a bodily function. However, each of the two has its own orientation.

It's A Balancing Act

Having this awareness, what can you do to increase your effectiveness in the goal setting process? Well, we know that there is a good and bad side to everything. Acting on situations with only one side of our brain exercises those characteristics that provide either a logical or creative view. This is simplifying things because both sides of our brain provide greater levels of support and functionality. However, the downside of this is not being able to create a balance between the two. Although you could function creatively in art, music and dance without the use of the left brain, most of our creativity requires a sound balance between intuition and logical thought. The same holds true for language and logic. Because the two are so rigidly organized, creative breakthroughs are difficult. You may have some indication as to what side of the brain you favor. It does not matter which side you prefer, make certain you try to create a balance in terms of how you view people and circumstances. The person who has a wholesome outlook on life accomplishes more than someone who is fatalistic and fearful that everyone is taking something away from him or is out to get him. Robert Schuller describes the difference between an optimist and a pessimist by noting that an optimist says "I'll see it when I believe it" and the pessimist says "I'll believe it when I see it." The optimist realizes the right attitude is critical in the goal setting process.

For example, if you prefer right brain thinking, you may find that you get overly emotional when things do not go as planned. You may take on a negative view of the situation and give up, looking only at the unpleasant aspects. If this is the case, try calling on the left brain functions and attempt to analyze the situation. Ask yourself these questions:

- ☐ What is the worst that could happen?
- ☐ What would I do if the worst happened?
- ☐ How can I recover from this right now?

Tune In, Don't Tune Out

Right brain people need to stop and analyze the situation. Applying some practical and logical steps to resolve it, could be the difference between your success and failure. In some cases, you may have exhibited body language that said more than you could ever verbalize and was also less than desirable. We remember these situations when they happen to us. They create mental pictures in our memory that are difficult to obliterate and easy to recall. In one unthinking, emotional moment, we destroy our chances for success. When you realize that the difference between success and failure is an inch or two, you will better understand how important it is to nurture a positive attitude. If success and failure can be measured in inches, then almost is not good enough. There is no joy in the promotion you almost got, the one-mile race you almost won, the vacation you almost took or the bar exam you almost passed.

Winners Never Lose

My niece and I were watching the news one evening when the sports segment came on. The sportscaster announced that a local bowling tournament was going to take place and mentioned the dollar amounts of the top three prizes. He said that the third place prize would be $6,000. My niece was overwhelmed that the person coming in last would get what she considered a lot of money for losing. I had to remind her of the disparities between winning and losing. I told her that there definitely are major differences, most of which have a lot to do with your attitude. People do not compete to lose. Think about it. Sugar Ray Leonard would not train for weeks prior to a major bout just to lose, telling himself, "Well, if I lose, at least I'll go home with 15 million dollars." He goes into every fight with a winner's attitude. He sees himself holding the belt high above his head in victory. I would bet that almost all professional athletes never, never, *ever* practice with the thought of losing. They do not go into competition thinking about what they will do with the silver or bronze. Carl Lewis does not think about it, neither does Orel Hershiser or Florence Griffith-Joyner. Not one of them ever entertained the thought of embracing the agony of defeat.

Left Brain Strategy

We have discussed how right-brainers can work towards changing attitudes. We will now look at a left-brainer's approach. Strategy for the left brain person is to make certain you do not get caught up in "analysis paralysis." Allow room for creativity as part of the sequential step-by-step approach to problem solving. Remember that if you took this same approach to programming a computer, it would not perform the specific task if one step was missing. The same may be true for the left brain individual. However, this would be reflected in your frustration with a situation when something was not in order or lacked any semblance of organization. There needs to be a balance between logic and creativity in order to package and sell your ideas. So, loosen up. If you find yourself being too rigid, ask yourself these questions:

☐ Do I consistently ask the five W's; Who?, What?, When?, Where?, and Why? and make people feel like they are on trial?

☐ Do people consider me the "Columbo" of the office, home, church, school, etc.?

☐ What would happen if I chose to respond with a statement instead of raising a question?

When you find yourself getting too serious and asking too many questions, turn the situation around. The next time this happens, respond with "Yes, last week, I was reading that in the *Journal*. Sounds like a dynamic project. I would love to work with that team." Although this may not be the appropriate reply, adjust your response to suit the situation. You will find that you are enjoying yourself more and allowing your creativity to shine through. Your attitude also has a lot to do with how people view you and how you view the world and those around you. Anyone who works with me or comes in contact with me on a regular basis will tell you that whenever they ask me how I'm doing I respond "Great!" I believe if I start the day off great, notwithstanding any major obstacles, the day will end great—or no less than good.

You're Okay, I'm Not

I used to work with a man who always responded "okay" when I inquired as to how he was doing. One day, my reply was, "You just feel okay?" He replied, "Yes, that way I leave room to feel better." Many of us can readily recall asking a co-worker or friend how they are doing and receiving a variety of responses: "Oh, not too bad for a Monday" or "It's too early to tell, check with me later," and "Seeing as how it's pay day, I'm doing fine," and the classic, "Is it time to go home yet?" Unfortunately, for many of these people, life is work. They become embarrassed when someone responds "Great" when asked how they are doing. For some reason, most individuals do not have a comfort level with that, perhaps because they do not believe anyone can have so much enthusiasm on a consistent basis.

Being enthusiastic comes naturally. You do not turn it on and off like a light switch. Elbert Hubbard said, "Nothing great has ever been accomplished without enthusiasm." It is a way of life and you do not avail yourself of it only on special occasions, when you are interviewing for a job or meeting your spouse's boss. Enthusiasm comes from within and reveals itself outwardly. By the same token, when you nurture a positive attitude, it helps to strengthen your mental and emotional powers. It is one of the most important elements in becoming a success.

Plant The Seed

When you nurture a positive attitude, you follow the same steps as you do when you plant seeds. You make certain you have proper soil and sunlight. This translates to positive thoughts and enthusiasm. You water the seedlings. This is akin to letting your positive thoughts flow freely. At maturation, you may do some pruning, which would be interpreted as enhancing or refining your attitude upwards. However, you must never dig up the seeds, because seeds dug up and inspected never develop to their true potential. This could come in the form of looking a gift horse in the mouth—questioning why you were promoted or given a new project over a more seasoned employee—or dwelling on mistakes and not allowing yourself to advance to the next logical step.

Your Emotional Roots

We know that everyone was not born with a positive attitude. Based on where you were raised and the approach your parents took in child rearing has a lot to do with how you view yourself and the world around you. When I was growing up, it seemed everyone had permission to discipline me. This included my teachers at school, the next door neighbor, elders at church, a relative or an older sibling. Not a day went by without someone admonishing me about not saying or doing something they felt was out of character for me.

Much of what was impressed upon me was in the form of verbal admonishments. If I was not getting a finger pointed in my face by my schoolteacher, one of the sisters in the church was warning me that if I did not stop running or talking, I was going to get a hand on my bottom.

As I matured, I realized how much of a negative impact it had on my personal relationships. Around the age of twenty, I decided to make a change in my attitude. At the time, my oldest brother was passionately involved with books, tapes and any motivational material he could get his hands on that supported his positive steps towards success. He shared every piece of literature with me. It did not take long for the bug to hit me and I followed his lead by reading books and listening to other motivational tapes that complemented his collection. I also attended seminars and workshops on personal development. I absorbed and retained almost everything and passed the information on to others who shared in my quest for original and positive information. Not only did I talk about it, I practiced what I preached.

Put The Blame On Me, Babe

I talk with many people about their goals and what they believe is standing in the way of their success. Together, we analyze their situations in an attempt to identify how attitude may hinder their progress. It is interesting how many people blame others for what happens to them. They blame their parents for not understanding them and for being too old-fashioned. They blame their spouses for being too insensitive. Many blame immigrants for doing quality work for less pay and still others put the blame on society in general. They never saw themselves as being responsible for their inability to be successful. They usually saw conditions or an individual as the showstopper. They did not see themselves as culpable. However, when you decide to fully take on a positive attitude, it means you take 100 percent responsibility for causing the effects in your life.

You are truly accountable and responsible for what happens to you and the onus starts and ends with you and no one else.

Sins Of The Parents

Not long ago, I had an opportunity to talk with my neighbor's teenage daughter. On this particular day, I spoke to her about school and asked how she was doing. She had just received her progress report and I asked if I could see it. When I took a look at it, I was startled to see the number of days tardy and absent, and that her grades were less than average. I inquired how many progress reports she received per school year. The report she showed me covered a period of six weeks, or thirty school days. During that time, she missed nine days of school and was tardy six times. Also, on three days out of the thirty school was closed for teacher conferences. This means the progress report revealed her scholastic aptitude for a total of twenty-seven days. My neighbor's daughter missed over 30 percent of that time. As far as I was concerned, this was astonishing. Being the inquisitive person that I am, I said, "Wow, you missed a lot of school; what happened?" She responded, "This always happens to me this time of year. I usually miss about eight days of school because I get the flu every year and mom makes me take time off." She went on to say, "I'm tardy a lot because my dad won't wake me up. He says, if I have an alarm clock I should get up when it goes off, but I keep telling him it's hard for me to do that, so I'm late for school sometimes." I could see that mom wanted me to continue, as she looked lovingly at her daughter. We talked quite some time and, to make a long story short, by the end of our conversation, her daughter had progressed from "I don't know" to "I did it because."

Several weeks later, I was returning home and saw my neighbor watering her lawn. I stopped by and asked how her daughter was doing in terms of her attitude and study habits. Mom replied: "I'm so pleased with her progress. She hasn't missed one day of school and hasn't been tardy, either." Mom added that her husband believed that, for the first time his daughter had accepted responsibilities for her actions.

Many of you have experienced a situation like my neighbor's and either dealt with it effectively or turned your back on it. Regardless of how you responded, your attitude had a lot to do with the success or failure of that situation. If you could alter the way you look at the following situations, what would you do differently to deal with each scenario:

- ☐ Your child's whining
- ☐ A negative performance appraisal from your boss
- ☐ Your spouse's inattentiveness
- ☐ Gossiping about friends and relatives
- ☐ Getting up in the morning to go to work
- ☐ Working late on an important project
- ☐ Lack of funds to pay bills and buy food

Knowing how your left and right brain function, how would you handle these situations?

Think about ways in which you can nurture that positive attitude just like the seedling I talked about planting. You can improve upon your lot and turn a negative attitude into a positive one.

I challenge you to stretch yourself in all aspects of your life. Enhance your positive attitude and cash in on the results which are abundant. Remain open to the challenges that present themselves to you. You will cut out a nice niche for yourself filled with many challenges and opportunities.

PART II

WHAT'S
IN A BRAIN

Knowledge fills a large brain; it merely inflates a small one.

—Sydney Harris

As human beings, we have two modes of perception and consciousness; the left and right sides of our brain. One side of the brain dominates the opposite side of the body. However, both sides work simultaneously and in parallel, to assist in dispatching mental, physical and emotional tasks. In that regard, we can consider ourselves both left- and right-brained, although we tend to favor one side over the other.

By design, various parts of the body comes in pairs; our thighs, hips, legs, arms, lungs, etc. The same is true for the brain. Each side is referred to as a hemisphere and controls and directs various aspects of our judgment, perception and rationale. The right side of the brain has its own train of thought and is considered the nonverbal or picturing side. The left side tends to think in words and is considered the verbal or logical side of the brain. The two sides have developed a partnership and work together to pass pictures, words and images between the two for verbal recognition and definition. Our brain works because both sides work simultaneously and in parallel.

Creative Juices At Work

In 1945, G. Wallas wrote a book, *The Art of Thought*, in which he divides the creative process into four phases: preparation, incubation, illumination and verification. He interpreted preparation as the gathering and isolating of pertinent information until all barriers are visible. During the incubation period, the unconscious processes of the mind have a tendency to work through the issue. However, there is no urgency to come to a solution. The illumination phase is more spontaneous. Intuition and insight are dominant and may produce solutions to the problem. Ultimately, the verification phase allows the intuitive solutions to be logically tested for validity then synthesized into some final solution. The first and last phases of this process are typical left brain tasks we have so comfortably employed for almost all problem solving processes. The real issue is that the two middle phases employ the use of the unconscious or right brain and are hardly ever used.

Our society and educational system are based almost exclusively on left brain thinking. We are asked to read, write and talk. Very seldom are we encouraged to commission right brain thinking to problem solve or as part of the learning process. Think about this for a moment: what is your preference for learning? Do you assimilate material more effectively through pictures, words or a combination of the two? Your choice and how you apply the two modes will define your ability to succeed in life. It is not enough to say you have a comfort level with one side over the other. Do not ever become satisfied with what you have accomplished in your life. You have an opportunity to draw upon existing resources that will help you enhance your techniques for accomplishing your goals. It has been said that we only use about 10 percent of our brain. However, once you learn to effectively tap the side you tend to neglect, you will increase your learning and problem solving capacity tenfold. A review of the left and right hemispheres reveals the following:

Left Hemisphere
Processes information in sequence
Connected to right side of body
Analytical thinking

Seat of reason
Logical
Rational
Specializes in memory recognition of words or numbers
Verbal/mathematical ability

Right Hemisphere

Processes information simultaneously
Connected to left side of body
Spatial orientation
Seat of passion and dreams
Pragmatic view
Depth perception
Specializes in memory recognition of places, persons, objects,
    music, etc.
Specializes in intuition

All this functionality is organized into three physical parts:
- □ Hindbrain
- □ Midbrain
- □ Forebrain

Hindbrain

This area is located at the back of the head, right above the ears.
Also known as the cerebellum, it is responsible for organizing our
body movements. Although you may not be aware of it, every time
you tap your toes or nod your head, this movement is controlled by
the hindbrain.

Midbrain

Located at the center of your head, the midbrain is comprised
mainly of nerve path fibers to and from the brain. It supports many
functions for the eye muscles and is responsible for movement of
the eyes and size of the pupils.

Forebrain

The forebrain is further divided into two sections, the hypothalamus and the thalamus; both are located above the midbrain. The hypothalamus behaves like a thermostat for the body. It regulates our sleep, metabolism, and sexual drive, as well as our appetite. It is about the size of a grape and is also considered a primitive part of the brain because it deals with such emotions as thirst, hunger and fear. On the other hand, the thalamus focuses on physical senses such as pain or temperature.

This knowledge about the brain helps explain its ability to manipulate our bodies in so many ways. We gain a better feel for how it orchestrates our thoughts and movements, our emotions and other senses. We could argue whether or not the brain and the mind are one and the same. Many experts on the subject have yet to agree on this issue. For all intents and purposes, the two terms are used synonymously.

Although there is a tendency to favor one side over the other, you limit yourself when you totally rely on properties of one side and ignore attributes of the other. When you use both sides together, you do not bank on the complete reasoning of one or the other to accomplish a goal. No matter how you develop and accomplish your goals, you order left and right brain rationale to achieve them. For example, your intuition, which is a right brain function, assists you with having foresight to view situations as they manifest themselves. Intuition can be a very powerful and guiding force, and using your intuition can heighten your goal-setting efforts.

Something Told Me To Do That

We are constantly besieged with gentle admonitions of the heart and spirit, but we generally don't heed them. There are reasons why you may ignore these little pushes. Sometimes, it is fear, doubt, listening to others, or just lack of faith. There are even those who close themselves off from accepting these prompts, saying to themselves, "This never happens to me," or "I don't get it." What usually happens is that everyone does receive these gentle prompts, but we struggle with whether or not we should follow them. Often, we end up doing just the opposite of what our "first mind" suggests, although in every situation, we regret having been so casual.

Left brain functions are used to document the step-by-step approach you generally take to problem solving. Although we may not be cognizant of it, we are comfortable with its application in terms of how it naturally influences our decisions.

First of all, you would enumerate the steps necessary to work through the problem either in your mind or by writing them down. With a little imagination you might come up with an alternate plan, in case your original strategy had some holes. Your approach may have been methodical and prompted you to divide each task into segments that could be resolved individually. Whatever the case, you took a step-by-step approach to solving the problem and called on left brain functions to accomplish it.

Analytical and logical reasoning lack luster without creative right brain forces. Conversely, intuition in and of itself is totally useless without left brain validation and verbal definition. Together, the left and right brain complement one another. In order to extract the maximum for both sides, make certain you understand how you currently use each side in problem solving and analytical reasoning. The next segment goes into more detail on how the sides differ and examines ways you can determine the side towards which you have a natural leaning.

VERBAL VS.
VISUAL THINKING

We know what a person thinks not when he tells us what he thinks, but by his actions.

—Issac Bashevis Singer

Statistics prove that most individuals who establish New Year's resolutions abandon them by the end of the first quarter. There is no single reason why this occurs; however, there is a direct correlation between written goals and success. As I mentioned in an earlier segment, a mere three percent of the population documents their goals on a regular basis. Although this figure may be startling, it underscores the necessity for individuals to put pen to paper and create some semblance of structure and direction in their lives. When you examine the lives of successful people, you will see a clear delineation of the things they want to achieve. I have talked with hundreds of them in their homes, at seminars, churches and meetings. There is one common thread that permeates their existence; at any given time, they can tell you where they are going, how they will get there and how long it will take them. They have discovered that in order to be a success, you must have a plan that comprises identifiable steps for achieving the stated success. A critical part of the equation is documenting that plan. This holds true for everyone.

It's Late Because I Procrastinate

You may find yourself drifting along without any focus or aim. You want to start working towards your goal, but somehow find yourself (once again) fidgeting, fumbling and fooling around. Of all the things we do to sabotage our efforts, procrastination is at the top of the list. Over 90 percent of the people I talk to about their goals admit to procrastinating. It is the single, most frequent complaint I hear and it does not discriminate based on gender. It is a part of human nature and everyone experiences it, at some level and at different times in their lives. For some, procrastination is factored into all things they undertake. They wait *until* the kids are in bed before they wash a load of clothes, or wait *until* their favorite television shows are over to pay bills. The problem with this approach is that typically, after the kids are in bed and their favorite TV shows are over, they are generally bushed and end up preparing themselves for bed. So, the task is put off yet another day. Other folks tell me they work better when they wait until the last minute, because it gives them a sense of urgency and they know that it *has* to be done "or else." Generally my question to them is, "Or else what? Or else you will lose your job, or else you will have your gas, lights or phone turned off, or else your kids will be disappointed in you?" You see, all these responses grow from excuses, which I outlined in another segment.

Reverse The Curse

It is important for you to realize that you can change the course of your life. It may take several attempts before you identify what you require to keep your efforts consistent and define the steps necessary to get things done. However, you can take advantage of the obstacles that stand in your way and build a stronger foundation. Some of you may realize that you need to get up one hour earlier than you normally do, others may need to get rid of extra baggage in their lives and eliminate affiliations with certain friends or relatives. You may need to spend more time by yourself, either at the start or end of the day. Whatever you decide, remember you can change the direction that you are headed. More importantly, start now and do not put it off any longer. Not long ago, a cousin said to me, "Erma, I always start projects I can't or don't finish. It's not that I'm not excited about the project but, I just don't keep the momentum going. What's wrong with this old man?" Initially, we joked about the aging process, but on a more serious note, I asked him how he went about working towards his goals. In other words, what is the first thing he does and the next and so on. Based on his feedback, I saw that he tends to verbalize his intentions more than acting on them. This happens to be the preferred method for most individuals. We think that talking about the things we want to accomplish will draw them closer and somehow magically make them appear. This could not be further from the truth. You must work through a well-documented plan. As you go through the process, take time to examine different facets of your personality and character to determine what makes you do the things you do. If you are being honest with yourself, you will identify what prevents you from being a success and seriously get back on track.

I See What I Want, I Say What I Need

I want to inspire you to start thinking about how you perceive situations and ultimately act on them. Your awareness of this process is a crucial ingredient in the goal setting process and invaluable in terms of deciding how to set your goals. Once you recognize how both sides of the brain operate, you will be better equipped to adjust the task to the approach. Let us begin with the left mode of thinking. We reviewed the functions of the left side of our brain in a previous segment. We determined that the left brain is verbal and:

- ☐ Analyzes and processes information sequentially, logically and analytically
- ☐ Is the seat of reason
- ☐ Left-brainers are good with words and comfortable expressing themselves verbally

This is simply an overview of the various left brain functions; other aspects were mentioned in a previous segment. However, if you lean towards left brain thinking, when establishing goals tap into the step-by-step logic that is inherent for left-brainers. Do not mislead yourself into thinking that because it is an intrinsic trait you will access it routinely.

A Natural Talent

Many of us are passive when it comes to exercising our inborn talents; notice I used the word talents. It is true that certain things are instinctive for some and learned skills for others. For example, the left brain specializes in musical ability and the right brain has a musical sense. While a left-brainer may be at home playing an instrument or singing, a right brain individual could learn to be musically inclined. So, just knowing that you are naturally inclined to the left, right or both sides will not guarantee success in any pursuit. What it will do, however, is provide you with a framework from which to build. It will help you determine your habitual approach to problems. It will be up to you to strengthen areas that are deficient and enhance what you consider to be your natural talents. Sometimes, we are called upon to provide snap decisions and contribute feedback based on some high level overview we receive involving pictures. When this happens, we may not be able to solicit questions about how information was captured. Neither can we say, "Let me get back with you on this." What is expected, however, is a prompt, concise and very close to accurate survey of the situation, including several suggestions for improvement.

Right And Left Field Of Dreams

Left-brainers may have difficulty assimilating the information and providing immediate feedback without first asking a series of questions. This allows them to have more of a comfort level with the information received as well as their responses. Without this additional feedback, the left-brainer could become frustrated and feel unable to offer any valuable input. So, what begins as a simple overview could result in a frustrating exercise in futility for someone who exercises left brain functions more readily.

The same scenario tendered to a right brain person could yield contrasting results. Because the right brain perceives information in a diffused manner, pictures, charts and graphs are a safe haven for right-brainers. These individuals comprehend information in an all-at-once or parallel manner. If you ask right brain people how they want to receive information, they would reply, "Bottom line me." They most likely respond "I see what you are saying," when asked if they understand something being presented to them. Ask that same question to left brain people and they might respond "I hear what you are saying." Because right-brainers are picturing people, they absorb information received from images and pictures like a sponge. When they establish goals, it is easier for them to picture themselves obtaining whatever they set out to accomplish.

If you are a right brain person, when you set goals, also construct a collage of the way you see your success. If your goals are to put a savings plan in motion, get a better job, have more income or a larger home, it will be helpful for you to cut out pictures of these items. Put them in an area you frequent so you can constantly view them. You may go as far as taking pictures with or next to these items so they become that much more of a reality for you. The pictures are not intended to take the place of documenting your goals. They are meant to complement the goals and help you visually draw them nearer.

The following is an example of how a right-brainer would pass pictures of their dream house over to the left brain for verbal definition:

My house has approximately 4,000 square feet of living space with high, beamed ceilings and hardwood floors. The kitchen has bay windows with a sitting area and all modern conveniences, including a large stainless steel refrigerator. In the summer, guests are entertained on the deck that spans the width of the house and has a customized grill. The deck flourishes with lots of plants and flowers. The master bedroom is on the first floor, with his and her closets, a spa tub with garden windows and a natural wood-burning fireplace. The basement extends the length of the house and includes a game room, kitchen, full bath, bedroom and exercise room.

Get the picture? Because you are a right brain individual, visualizing your dream is almost effortless for you. Remember that although you see the picture, you need to make certain you document your goals too. Because you prefer things at a high level and have a tendency to see the whole picture, you may not see the need or value in documenting your goals. This could work against you and may prevent you from ever taking the time to include this crucial step. However, once you are familiar with the techniques and decide to make a commitment to document your goals, place a lot of emphasis on the use of pictures and images.

Left-brainers are more inclined to be analytical, taking a systematic approach to goal setting. While you may not have as much difficulty embracing the concept of documenting your goals, you may get into too much detail and overstate your goals and objectives. There is a natural tendency for you to overanalyze things, sometimes to a fault. Go ahead and state what you want to do, including your objectives. But, take care not to try and figure out every possible angle. As a left-brainer, you can learn a lot from your right brain companions. A good example would be to take a more creative approach to accomplishing your goals. Instead of trying to figure out all the details, allow yourself to decide the outcome of an objective as you work towards its completion. Try asking a teenager or someone much younger than yourself how they would work through the issue. That approach would be more creative.

There are other right and left brain qualities with their own unique characteristics. The left brain is crucial for mathematicians and scientists, while the right brain is the side critical for artists and craftsmen. You can motivate and inspire yourself to greater levels of accomplishment when you use each attribute appropriately.

These comparisons are not meant to contend that one side of the brain is superior to the other. The intent is to uncover traits of the right and left brain to provide you with sensible techniques for working through your goals. Each technique contributes to a carefully laid out method for accomplishing the goal. The objective is to select aspects from the side of the brain you tend to neglect and accentuate those features in order to complement the exploited side. Once you familiarize yourself with left and right brain functions, it is easy to learn to develop a goal mind.

CHAPTER SEVEN

GENDER
DIFFERENCES

*Some of our
best men are
women.*

—United States Army

No doubt, men and women are different. For over a hundred years, scientists have made an attempt to explain those differences. In every aspect of life, men and women seem to behave differently or perform similar functions in dissimilar ways. Women are more intuitive and better-equipped to notice things to which men are relatively oblivious. Men, on the other hand, have better spatial ability. They picture things, their shape, position, geography and proportion with greater accuracy, in their minds eye. Women have solid language skills and perform better than men on tests of verbal ability. Mathematically, men outperform women in their ability to resolve abstract concepts of space relationships and theory. There is, however, one common trait they share; they come from the same species. Aside from the physical aspects, the primary reason men and women are different is that anatomically and structurely, their brains are different.

Send A Woman To Do A Man's Job?

It was of utmost importance, during the feminist movement of the '70s, for women to demonstrate they could perform the same physical tasks as men. The issue at hand was a woman's right to earn equal pay for equal work. There was progress, and some women earned the right to perform jobs traditionally held by men. That movement provided women the impetus to aspire to lofty achievements and for men to gain greater knowledge of women's physical and intellectual abilities. But the bucks did not stop there. For more than two decades, there has been an enormous amount of research conducted on the dissimilarities between the sexes. There is now less speculation about the differences and the methods by which the sexes become different. Research reveals two contradictory processes, however; the scientific research into the differences and the political denial that they exist. For the most part, interest in the differences originally stemmed from scientific motives to suppress them, beginning with IQ tests. In about thirty of the abilities tested, researchers consistently saw disparities that favored one sex over the other. Dr. D. Wechsler and other reseachers sought to resolve the issue by obliterating all tests that showed these significant differences. When that proved fruitless, they deliberately instituted male or female specific elements to come up with approximately like scores. This fudging of the numbers is an odd way of conducting scientifc research. It suggests that if you do not get the results you want, you simply alter the data to produce more favorable results.

What's Wrong With Being Different?

The differences in male and female brains occur in the hours immediately following birth. We now know that as infants, girls are interested in people and faces, and boys are content having an object swinging in front of them.

A friend of mine and her husband are in the process of remodeling their kitchen. They have gone to great lengths to employ the best labor and have haggled over price, materials and other deliverables. They have been at it for several months. One of the most intriguing aspects of their venture is how each values different components of the project. As an example, Ellen is concerned with aesthetics, lighting and the ergonomic flow, in terms of how many twists and turns she must make to get from one appliance to the next. She is also thinking about how much room friends and relatives will have when she hosts a party. After all, this is where people congregate when you have a party, right? On the other hand, Kevin's focus is with the plumbing, budgetary constraints and blueprints. His concerns are what he may describe as practical and no-nonsense. No matter how many people can fit into the kitchen, if the plumbing's installed incorrectly they may end up all wet. Ellen's interests are visual and compassionate, or the touchy-feely things that affect the right brain. So there. We have a left and right brain view. Both are correct and add value to the project. The bottom line is, there is nothing wrong with being different. We should applaud gender differences and work towards blending unique aspects from both sides to create a balance that allows us to derive the most good from them. Men with greater spatial abilities and women with superior language skills can coexist rather effectively. We should allow men to figure out which route to take on the family vacation, and the best way to solve spatial problems, but let the women explain it to everyone else.

Tell Me What's On Your Mind

Since the beginning of time, perhaps, women have felt that men do not listen to them. Talk shows are filled with experts recommending ways for women to maximize on what some women refer to as the one-way communications they have with their spouses and lovers. And women have gone to great lengths to get their point across. Women attest to whispering, crying, screaming, shouting and sometimes feigning illness, all in the name of communicating their feelings. The answer to: "How can I get my husband/lover to listen to me?" lies in the way men and women use their heads to communicate. Research shows women use left and right brain functions for language, while men use only the left side. Since the right side controls emotions and the left side verbal skills, women are better equipped to transfer their emotions or feelings to the left side of their brain for verbal recognition and definition. This does not mean a man cannot communicate what is on his mind. It simply means that the communication is usually not tied to a great deal of emotion. For many women, this proves to be the most frustating aspect of their relationships. They ask their partner to share his deepest feelings, but men have been conditioned not to express their feelings. It is the "don't cry unless you have an onion under your nose" syndrome.

You Just Wait, I'll Show You How I Feel

Some researchers believe men have a greater capacity to feel than most women. They say a mans reluctance to communicate his feelings is biologically rooted. The emotional center of his brain is located in a different area than a woman's. In other words, he is not holding things in, he just does not call on these emotions as frequently as a woman. However, when he does, he communicates through physical courtesies like buying gifts and flowers, or asking his mate to go on a special outing. When a man opens your car door, gives you his jacket on a brisk night, calls you in the middle of the day or carries in the groceries for you, he is saying he cares. Although the woman would prefer a verbal demonstration of his feelings because it is the intimacy a woman longs for in a relationship. There is a lesson to be learned from this; respect the methods men use to communicate their feelings. When you pour out your heart to him and he holds you closer and responds "yeah," take that as a clear signal of his true affection for you. And when he shares that rare moment with you and cannot stop expressing himself, do not spoil the moment by responding, "Oh, so you're not a vegetable after all." I had an opportunity to see a friend from college recently and she was saddened by the direction her marriage had taken over the past five months. She explained that no matter how hard she tried, she could not get her husband to express his feelings. She said, "Whenever he does talk for long periods of time, it's with friends and relatives. He never shares that much stuff with me and it drives me crazy, because I want to know what he's thinking." I told her it sounds like the things he shares with friends and relatives are topical, not the intimate things she wants him to share with her. He gets excited about talking shop, cars and sports with his friends. When it comes time to discuss matters of the heart, the emotion is still there, but at a different level. I suggested she consider this in future conversations and try phrasing statements so they are open ended and more light-hearted. This may not change the fact that male brains are programmed for action rather than people. But, when discussing various topics, try keeping the statements short. Do not give a dissertation about something and at the very end ask him "What do you think?" Because you can expect a more abbreviated response than yours and this may get your water boiling. If your statements and his responses are short, accept that as a gift and do not look the gift horse in the mouth. Of course, if it requires a more detailed explanation, by all means, probe. But proceed with diplomacy.

Pardon Me, May I Scan Your Gray Matter?

Most experts agree there is a slight difference in the structure of women's and men's brains. But the studies have been inconclusive on whether the anatomical disparities make them think differently. With new technologies like positron emmision tomography, or PET scans, and functional magnetic resonance imaging (FMRI), researchers are able to watch the brain thinking, feeling and recollecting. Men and women were PET-scanned while solving math problems, figuring out rhymes, thinking idly and judging facial expressions. Although the research is early at this point, there is data to support the idea that men and women in general have brains that work differently. Studies conducted in 1995 reveal male and females show various levels of intense activity in certain parts of the brain when performing different functions. Brains of men with high SAT scores seemed to work harder than mathematically gifted women with comparable scores. Richard Haier is professor of pediatrics and neurology at the University of California, Irvine, and leader of SAT studies in men and women. He PET-scanned 22 male and 22 female volunteers while they worked through SAT math problems. Half the men and half the women had scores above 700. The other half scored around 540. His unpublished results show that the temporal lobe, the area behind the ears, was "on overdrive" for the men, but the same area for women showed little activity. Haier says "There was a suggestion that women who did better in math might be using their brains more efficiently than women who did average." Even when asked to think of nothing, 13 men and 4 women showed activity more like the other sex's. The PET scan showed that when asked to think of nothing, men fixated on sex and football and women on strings of words. In February of 1995, researchers also announced information that men and women use different parts of their brains to figure out rhymes. Nineteen men and women were tested. In all 19 men an area of the front left side of their brains lit up like a Christmas tree when figuring out whether or not words like lete and jete, loke and joke rhymed. In 11 of the women that same area and the area behind the right eybrow were active. However, in eight of the women, or 42 percent, their brains worked like those of the men.

Different, Smifferent

These findings should not impose an intellectual threat to either gender. Nor should they be construed to imply males are superior to females or vice versa. We agree that the sexes are different even if we can predict hostility from folks who think the differences are a by-product of social conditioning. Boys and girls behave differently from birth and society's imprint could not be so instaneous. So women are more sensitive than men to sound, smell, taste and touch. They are more attuned to facial expressions and gestures and process sensory and verbal information faster. Men are more agressive and self-assertive and are better at skills requiring spatial ability. Anne Moir, Ph.D and David Jessel, authors of the controversial national best-seller *Brain Sex* say, "Men need the hierarchy and rules, for without them they would be unable to tell if they were on top or not—and that is of vital importance to most men." As individuals, we should recognize that men and women have competencies that contrast with one another. No matter what is stated in the Declaration of Independence, all things are not created equal. The Creator exquisitely designed man and other living things to be alike in form but different in their internal and external design. Our focus should not be on what the differences are, but how one complements the other. As researchers uncover new aspects of male and female brain differences, the information should be brought to the table, published and celebrated. If we choose to ignore the differences we run the risk of believing all men and women are equally competent in every aspect of life. When all is said and done, we can only hope that men and women will stop trying to be what the other sex wants them to be, and become content being themselves.

USE IT
OR LOSE IT

Our body thrives on challenges and workouts. When we develop ourselves physically, we grow and become more powerful, flexible and alert. The same is true for our brain. Our intelligence increases and becomes more robust and agile with regular workouts. In fact, over the past twenty years, experiments have been conducted with animals that suggest this is true. The experiments imply that the structure of cells in the brain's cortex changes physically as a result of sustained intellectual activity. If we link the results of these findings on animals with humans, it becomes clear that accountability for the development of our brain lies within us.

The question then is, how do we begin to exercise our intelligence? What steps can we take on a day-to-day basis to strengthen our intellect? Dr. Howard Gardner, a Harvard psychologist, divides intelligence into the following seven categories:

Linguistic skills
Logical-mathematical skills
Musical skills
Spatial skills
Bodily and kinesthetic skills
Interpersonal skills
Intrapersonal skills

Applying Your Intellect

A large percentage of us employ all these skills daily, but few of us to the same degree. Just as we have a tendency to regularly exercise one side of our brain over the other, we do the same with our intellectual skills. While we may not give equal attention to all seven skills, we can make an effort to ensure no one skill is completely ignored. For example, when examining an article that is technically oriented, the intellectual reader may stop after three paragraphs to review what he just read. In his mind, he fully understands what he studied but he initiates a series of "what if's" to determine other consequences to the narrative. By going through this exercise the reader begins to stretch his imagination. This approach allows him to perceive the written information and deduce several other conclusions based on his ability to apply critical reasoning.

These differences exhibit the distinction between two mindsets. In one case, the individual questions what has been read, seeking additional meaning. This is someone who reads between the lines; someone who is moderately philosophical in his approach to evaluating the written and spoken word. More than likely, this individual would call your attention to an article he thought was interesting. He may pause at a certain point and say "listen to this," hoping to engage in stimulating and lively conversation that encourages analytical reasoning.

Repeat After Me ...

On the other hand, someone who is considered knowledgeable may not question what is presented, whether written or spoken. He has an affinity for accepting the status quo. This person is what some folks refer to as a walking encyclopedia. If reciting various parts of history, this person may not have much insight into the politics of a particular event. He will, however, wax enthusiastic over date-driven, time-sequenced events. The unfortunate thing is that dialogue with this individual is one-dimensional. He usually can tell you what but not why. When asked why a particular event occurred, he is apt to respond "Well, they say it may have been due to . . ." but provide none of his own conclusions or convictions. When you stretch your mental capacity and challenge your problem solving skills, you will not allow ourselves to become mentally malnourished.

Why Do Birds Suddenly Appear?

You can start now to augment your problem solving capacity. Take, for example, dialogue between two people. The topic is bird-watching. This may be an uninteresting subject to you and, if on the receiving end, you may find yourself becoming a passive listener.

But, how many times have you observed birds flying in various patterns and wondered why? Did you question it by getting a book on the subject? Did you ask someone's opinion? You may have thought that certain times of the year, there are specific patterns the birds fly in, but you did not inquire. However, if you raised any of these questions, it suggests your desire to cultivate the ability to analyze and reason through various situations. If you are not doing this now, start preparing yourself by asking questions.

Step Outside The Box

You can expand your intellectual powers by stepping outside the box and questioning situations you do not grasp as readily as others. You should also challenge the rules you have set for yourself. Edwin Land took a picture of his daughter one day on an outing in 1943. He became annoyed when she asked why she could not see the picture "now" and got the idea for the Polaroid camera. Step outside your usual mode of operation and go about things differently. Recently, I was discussing a potential problem with my assistant. During the course of the conversation, she asked me, "Erma, what can we do?" I replied, "Well, we could kick, laugh, scream, cry, pray, talk about it some more, eat a banana. There's a lot of things we can do." She began to laugh heartily. I asked her what was so funny. She said that as I began to enumerate the various things we could do, she began to get a picture in her mind of how we would look doing each of them. We discussed each of them for a while and although we got off the track a bit, it was stimulating to take a different perspective and return to the problem with a fresh outlook.

Do not allow yourself to be one-dimensional in terms of the way you view life and your interaction with folks. It is so easy to get into a pattern. Go ahead and try things you normally view as something for the "other guy." The mother-in-law of a friend told me she never liked crossword puzzles or word search games. I spent some time with their family one Christmas and one of her grandchildren received a Scrabble game. The entire time everyone played the game, grandma shouted out responses to assorted questions raised by others. This happens to many of us in a variety of different areas. We passionately claim our disdain for a particular subject or activity but when someone else is thoroughly enjoying it, we want to get involved.

There are many things you can do to expand your mental horizons. Try flying a kite the way it should be flown, or sitting on the kitchen floor and playing jacks. How about saying some of the most challenging tongue twisters? Allow yourself to put together a model kit or take several hundred pictures without worrying about the cost. Use your brain more effectively for problem solving and for simple tasks in order to stretch it to its fullest potential. When you step outside the box and approach life more creatively, you will expand your mental capabilities.

HEADING IN THE
RIGHT DIRECTION

Man's mind, stretched to a new idea, never goes back to its original dimension.

—Oliver Wendell Holmes

This segment is devoted to providing exercises that will assist you in maximizing your whole brain. Activities are intended to determine how you currently utilize your left and right brain and are divided into two sections:

□ **Identify**
□ **Clarify**

Identify – In order to begin working on enhancing your brain power, you need to have a point of reference. These exercises are designed to help you recognize how you currently use your mind.

Clarify – The purpose of this section is to interpret your answers for each exercise and determine whether or not you lean more towards left or right brain thinking.

Work through every exercise in the order given because each builds upon the next.

IDENTIFY:
EXERCISE 1—Analytical Reasoning

On a separate sheet of paper give yourself **25 minutes** to answer the following questions:

1. WARM is to HOT as COSTLY is to:

      a. pay   b. food   c. exorbitant

      d. tepid   e. price

2. SEED is to PLANT as CHILD is to:
    - a. boy
    - b. play
    - c. mother
    - d. adult
    - e. toy

3. LAKE is to POND as MANSION is to:
    - a. home
    - b. money
    - c. water
    - d. bricks
    - e. dwell

4. Which word below belongs with the following words:
    TRACK, PATH, COURSE
    - a. success
    - b. direction
    - c. right
    - d. angle

5. FATHER is to DAUGHTER as GRANDFATHER is to:
    - a. aunt
    - b. grandmother
    - c. sister
    - d. teacher
    - e. mother

6. Which word does not belong with the others?
    - a. frequently
    - b. probably
    - c. rarely
    - d. never
    - e. always

7. BED is to SLEEP as CHAIR is to
    - a. rest
    - b. dream
    - c. sit
    - d. health
    - e. weariness

8. TABLE is to LEG as BED is to
    - a. plate
    - b. knee
    - c. tail
    - d. cube
    - e. mattress

9. GLOVE is to BALL as HOOK is to
    - a. fish
    - b. game
    - c. stadium
    - d. bait
    - e. weather

10. FAIL is to SUCCEED as RIGHT is to
      a. high   b. sight   c. tide
      d. way   e. wrong

11. CUP is to DRINK as PLATE is to
      a. supper   b. eat   c. bowl
      d. fork   e. saucer

12. TUNE is to DEAFNESS as COLOR is to
      a. hearing   b. light   c. ear
      d. blindness   e. blue

13. SOAP is to DIRT as ERASER is to
      a. trash   b. detergent   c. water
      d. pencil   e. book

14. GUN is to SHOOTING as BOOK is to
      a. library   b. tearing   c. worm
      d. reading   e. shelf

15. WATER is to DRINK as FOOD is to
      a. sleep   b. walk   c. eat
      d. take   e. cooler

EXERCISE 2—Numerical Reasoning

For each question, select the number that would be next in the series.

1. 1, 4, 7, 10, 13, 16, ___
2. 3, 6, 10, 15, 21, 28, 36, ___
3. 5, 9, 13, ___, 21, 25, 29
4. 0, ___, 34, 51, 68
5. 1, ___, 10, 16, 23, 31
6. 4, 6, ___, 14, 28, 30, 60
7. 3, 5, 8, 12, ___, 23, 30

8. 1, ___, 6, 12, 36, 72, 216
9. ___, 10, 13, 23, 36, 59
10. 3, 4, 4, 6, 12, ___, 45, 49
11. 12, 6, ___, 18, 324, 162
12. 2, 28, 4, 24, 6, ___, 8, 16
13. 2, 3, 3, 5, 10, 13, 39, ___
14. 33, 28, 24, ___, 19, 18, 18
15. 2, ___, 9, 18, 19, 38, 39, 78

Before you continue, take some time to relax your mind. Do not review your answers. For the next two to five minutes, just sit quietly. When you have completed this rest period, proceed to the next exercise.

EXERCISE 3—Spatial Orientation

Allow yourself **ten** minutes to complete the following exercise. Complete the symbolic series for each of the following patterns

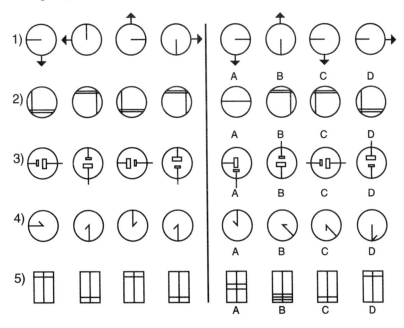

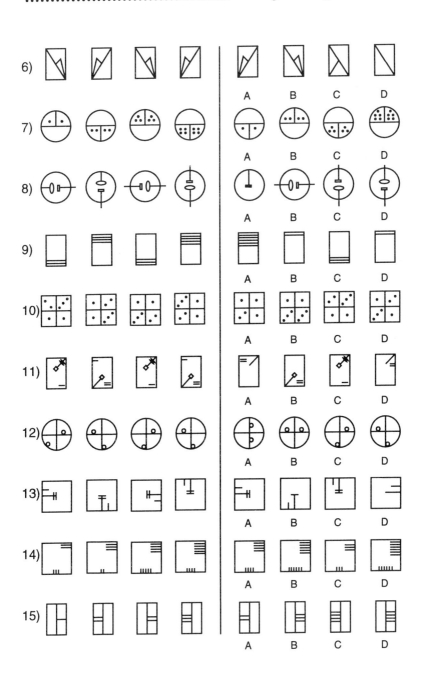

CLARIFY:
EXERCISE 1

     1. C   2. D   3. A   4. B   5. E
     6. D   7. C   8. E   9. A   10. E
     11. B   12. D 13. D 14. D 15. C

EXERCISE 2

     1. 19   2. 45   3. 17   4. 17   5. 5
     6. 12   7. 17   8. 2   9. 3   10. 15
     11. 36 12. 20 13. 42 14. 21 15. 8

EXERCISE 3

     1. C   2. C   3. C   4. C   5. D
     6. B   7. D   8. B   9. C   10. C
     11. C 12. C 13. A 14. D 15. B

Your Results
EXERCISE 1

1 – 5   Identifying up to five answers in this exercise demonstrates a sense of analytical judgment, but not very strong. However, don't give up. You can become more adept at this type of logic. All you need is practice. Obtain additional books and material on how to best use your analytical skills.

6 – 10   You have a higher comfort level with analytical reasoning and logic. While you may not be utilizing your left brain functions as effectively as you could, with more practice you will strengthen your skills in this area.

11 – 15 You are truly at ease exercising skills in analytical and logical rationale. You are utilizing left brain facilities in a most effective way. Continue to stretch your skills in this area by practicing different types of verbal analogies.

EXERCISE 2

1 – 5   Your feel for mathematical logic and reasoning is low for these types of models. In order to expand your aptitude in this area, purchase books that assist in developing your level of awareness and expertise.

6 – 10   You are good at recognizing this type of mathematical pattern and series. You could improve in this area by devoting additional time to this and other mathematical models.

11 – 15   Your comprehension of this type of mathematical pattern and series is high. Whether you got all correct or missed a few, take additional time to continue to practice these and other models in order to stay sharp by utilizing your left brain faculties.

EXERCISE 3

1 – 5   Your score reveals a low to medium skill set in the area of spatial orientation. You can improve your ability to recognize these and other types of spatial relations if you obtain additional materials to assist you in this area and practice these and more complex relations.

6 – 10   You have a medium to high skill level in this area. Just as I recommended for other exercises, get other material that will help you improve your knowledge base in these and more complex spatial relations.

11 – 15   You are good with understanding a variety of spatial concepts and relations. Although you scored high, you should continue to review additional books on how to get even better in this area.

Overall Results

These exercises were intended to give you some indication of how you currently utilize your left and right brain. Depending on how you scored, i.e. 11 – 15 for exercise one and 1 – 5 for exercise three, the results help you evaluate to what extent you employ these faculties. The exercises are in no way intended to determine your IQ. Additionally, there are other aspects of the brain that are not uncovered by working through these exercises.

No matter what your results, it is entirely up to you to make certain you continue to stretch both sides of the brain. Do not allow yourself to become content.

MIND
OVER MATTER

As children, our developmental process is influenced by our parents, teachers, neighbors and friends. We are conditioned and socialized to behave certain ways. On a regular basis, parents tell their sons not to cry or show their emotions, to be "a man." Mothers admonish their daughters to behave like a "little lady." We may not realize that no matter how well intended, this constant urging formulates an indelible impression in our minds. As we mature and experience life, there are countless opportunities to trigger that behavior.

The subconscious mind has no way of distinguishing between what is real or false, fiction or fantasy. Whatever messages you convey, verbal or imagined, are imprinted on your subconscious mind. They come so frequently and involuntarily that most of us pay little or no attention to them. However, you can control the frequency and random nature of these thoughts and benefit from them.

Dirty, Rotten Thoughts

Have you ever had an extreme departure from a simple thought? For instance, you begin thinking about the whereabouts of your child's school bus. You have been at the bus stop for ten minutes longer than usual. You think to yourself, "The bus has always been here on time. I hope nothing is wrong." Taking that fleeting thought, you begin to think, something could be wrong, and introduce a whole series of thoughts, all of which are negative in design and in terms of how they make you feel. The next thing you know, you picture yourself calling a relative or friend, frantically relaying the horrible details of how the bus was in an accident and your child was hurt. You may have taken it to the point of living the entire hospital emergency room scene and even buried the poor child. Now, please do not laugh and say to yourself this is a gross exaggeration, because it is not. It is an example of how we allow ourselves to get carried away with our thoughts. We can all honestly say we have taken a brief thought and elaborated on its contents. We do it to the point of believing it actually occurred or that it has the potential to develop. And because the mind cannot discern the difference between fact or fantasy, we conclude the picture is real.

Weighty Thoughts

Imagine being able to think about something and it materializes. When you weigh the number of negative, pointless and injurious thoughts that may cross our minds daily, the results could be astounding. I believe anyone endowed with that amount of control would be considered immeasurably destructive. This is just one side of the coin. You may recall having a thought that later reveals itself. It could have taken a day, year or month—or perhaps less. Have you ever thought about someone and they phoned you? Or thought aloud and someone said, "I was just thinking about that?" Well, both situations show only a portion of the full potential and power of our minds. The same energy that generates these thoughts can be redirected to help you overcome obstacles and triumph over any hurdles in life. The secret to tapping into this power is you must allow it to happen and not fight the thoughts that initially enter your mind. The first instance that you entertain a thought about a situation, it is usually accurate. You often can characterize these thoughts by how fleeting they tend to be. There is a saying: your first mind never leads you wrong. I used to hear this quite often as a child. Over the years, I have learned to trust my instincts and have allowed them to lead me to making the right decisions for myself and my family.

Cultivate Your Intuition

As you establish goals for yourself, you will need to exercise this same source of spiritual energy. Do it by using your gut level intuition and working hard to develop a trust in your feelings. Cultivating faith in your inner self demonstrates your ability to overcome mind over matter. Just understand that the concept of goal setting is simple in design but complex in application. You must learn to overcome any roadblocks that may hinder your ability to have total control over your mental rationale. Many workshop participants tell me the toughest thing they face that requires them to exercise mind over matter deals with drinking, eating or smoking. The thought process works this way: You decide on a goal you want to attain; in your mind, you may work through it and even welcome the challenge. Initially, you may feel motivated to work towards the completion of your goal. Sometime later, the thought crosses your mind again and you realize you have not started working towards the goal. Somehow, you cannot seem to muster the same level of energy you had when you originally decided upon this option. Part of this may be due to not taking the time to write down what you want to do. There is something quite fulfilling about documenting the things you want to accomplish. Imagine being able to pick up a piece of paper and say to yourself, "This is what I want to do and this is how I'm going to go about doing it." You would be amazed at the positive effects it has on your psyche.

Silent Messages

Remember, we constantly send messages to our mind that help determine our successes or failures in life. For example, you decide to make a commitment to spend more time with your family. You discuss this with your spouse and children and plan to start immediately. However, prior to putting any real effort into the plan, you begin to experience doubtful feelings about it. These feelings turn into negative thoughts that, in turn, make an impression on your subconscious mind. You may begin to imagine your children fussing during these "quality" periods, or envision your spouse being aloof. As a result of these thoughts, you tell yourself, this was not a good idea, it probably will not work, no one else cares. The impact of these thoughts, however, will drive you to behave in a manner that confirms your thoughts. So, we need to become more aware of the power of the mind and our capacity to control it. The things we have been conditioned to believe motivate us to behave in ways that help or hinder us.

The Blame Game

Every day, you have opportunities to exercise mind over matter. You make up your mind to take action on a given situation. No one makes up your mind for you. Although you may say others made you do a particular thing, this is not true. People may provide feedback and insight, but it is up to you to make the final decision. It is you who makes up your mind to watch your intake of calories and you who makes up your mind to exercise, be a better parent or get a better paying job. There are times when folks point to others after they make a bad decision. They wallow in their inadequacies and say they made the decision because someone told them to do it. However, these folks would be wise to realize it is they, not others, who are to blame for the good and bad in their lives. There are some folks who think luck has a lot to do with success and accomplishing goals. They think it has something to do with the day and time they were born or their horoscope. The reality is, in order to be a success at any one thing, you must have some sense of order. In other words, you must be disciplined. Let me reiterate my previous statement about goal setting. Reaching your goals is simple in concept but complex in application.

Distractions, Obstacles and Frustrations— Let Me Count The Ways

When I began writing the first edition of this book, the toughest thing for me to do was set aside a few hours daily to work on it. At the time, my business was home-based and there were many distractions. My office was in the loft and every sound coming up from the family room appeared to occur right next to me. My son always wanted extra hugs and kisses whenever I turned on the computer. The television seemed to be on nonstop. There was clattering and clanging of dishes and questions asked of others that I felt compelled to answer or question. In spite of every possible distraction, I forged ahead, promising myself I would try and complete at least three pages each evening. Sometimes, when I went to bed, I was mentally exhausted from trying to create a division between the distractions and my creativity. What kept me going all those nights? For one thing, I was determined to make this goal a habit. Whenever I sat down at the computer, I had no idea whether or not I would complete three pages. I had never written a book before. At the time, I was uncertain whether the three-pages-per-night goal was too lofty. My main objective was to see if I could discipline myself to spend two hours every night on the computer. I knew if I were consistent, my efforts would pay off. The day came when I was able to hold a manuscript in my hand. On that day, I was able to begin contacting people in the publishing industry about my book. So, no matter what level of frustration I met, I continued on with the stated goal and was able to achieve it within the time frame I had documented earlier. And the real difference between those who do what they set out to do and those who don't? It is simple. They just do it. It is really nothing more than that. Honestly. For me, there is no fun in getting up at 4:40 every morning to exercise. The real joy comes after I have completed the thirty-minute routine and check off another day on my calendar. That is when I get the rush. As I walk past the mirror and give myself another thumbs up, I truly understand what it takes to overcome mind over matter. I can also appreciate the difficulties, complexities and challenges associated with it.

Out Of Nowhere, You Find The Strength

We have heard the story of the mom who lifted the car from her trapped child. Many of us may want to believe she got the strength "out of nowhere." However, this is not the case. The strength was always there, waiting to be drawn upon, to be used to its fullest potential. All of us have that strength within us. That energy, if tapped regularly, can create a stream of emotion-rich enthusiasm that will carry us through any obstacle. You may not find yourself lifting cars, bending silverware with the slightest touch of your hand or recovering from a near death experience. You will find numerous opportunities to improve upon your lot. It will be entirely up to you to decide whether or not you can focus your efforts to the point of conquering mind over matter. I will not tell you it is going to be easy. I mean it when I say achieving a goal is complex in terms of its application. It is always easy to say what you are going to do. Putting substance behind the words and practicing what you preach is the most challenging, yet rewarding, aspect of goal setting.

Whistle While You Work

Recently, I spoke with my younger brother. He shared a concern of his regarding his personal life. As we talked, he seemed to become more and more disheartened. I asked him to reverse the situation and think of what else could have happened. After assessing the potential impact of some of the "what if" scenarios, he realized that things were not as rotten as they seemed. We talked for a few minutes longer and he mentioned that he was going to walk the dog. I asked him to whistle when he went for his walk. I asked him to do this because it is pretty difficult to be angry or sad while you whistle. You have to try awfully hard. Besides, when you whistle, chances are you will not whistle a sad tune. You may sing a sad song, but chances are you would not think of whistling one. Think about it the next time you are feeling a bit melancholy. This is just another simple exercise in conquering mind over matter.

This suggestion will help him refocus his attention from his apparent disappointment. Whistling will free his mind of negative thoughts. He will then be prepared to receive the key required to unlock the treasure chest of solutions waiting to be tapped. Just like my brother, that chest will provide you with the internal strength needed to overcome obstacles. Once you unlock your potential, there is nothing you cannot achieve.

PART III

HOW TO ACHIEVE
YOUR GOALS

Pick battles big enough to matter, small enough to win.

—Jonathan Kozol

Sometimes it is reasonable for us to assume that in order to accomplish a task we can simply think about it, get up and begin working on it. This is true for very rudimentary tasks such as washing dishes, or making phone calls. However, when attempting to accomplish anything of any magnitude (for some of us, washing dishes is), it is very important that we C.H.A.R.T.© a course of action. Deciding what it is you want to do and how you will set out to accomplish it is part of the motivating factor in goal setting. Before you get started, you need to know your point of reference. In other words, identify where you stand today. Are you satisfied with your successes? If not, ask yourself what you need to do to turn that around. What adjustments in your personal, spiritual, or physical lifestyle would you need to aspire to in order to raise your level of satisfaction? Would it be a more rewarding job? Perhaps owning a business would do it. For some, it may be spending more time with your family. You can make that decision for yourself. Take time to document what you want out of life. Ask yourself how hard you are willing to work for what you want. Are you ready to sacrifice some of your leisure time?

Get Busy, But Take Baby Steps

Whatever course of action you decide, you will need to get busy and stay busy. You will not make a complete turnaround overnight.

Remember, you were used to doing other things in your spare time. This adjustment will require a firm commitment on your part. Be aware that even though you have good intentions, you can get off track. As an example, if you wanted to put a savings plan in motion, you can rest assured that as soon as your savings reach an all time high, there will be countless reasons why you should dip into your stash and spend just a bit. One reason could be that you've had a bad day. You may feel that you owe yourself a nice dinner, or perhaps your child has done well at school, so you want to shower him with trinkets. Believe me, the list is virtually endless. Whatever the reason, do not give in to temptation. Try to exercise control. By the way, if a new savings plan is your goal, remember to start small. Promise yourself that the first thing you will do when you get paid is write a check with *your* name on it and deposit it in your account. In other words, always pay yourself first. I can remember opening a savings account with the credit union. I was a teenager at the time and was excited about joining the credit union's Christmas Club. It didn't take long for me to get used to them deducting $10 from my weekly check. Because I took baby steps, I was successful at saving over $500 in one year. This same approach can work for you, but you must get busy. I do not mean you must get busy thinking. You must get busy doing.

Self-Imposed Obstacles

During the process of working through the achievement of your goals, obstacles will present themselves; some are self-imposed and others are brought on by others. Let us first deal with those we introduce. When we make a decision to accomplish a task, we generally have good intentions. In other words, we do not say to ourselves, "Let me see if I can louse this up." But somehow, we get off track and begin to allow ourselves to fall into the I'll-do-it-tomorrow mode. When we do this, we end up standing in our own way. Most of us would not agree with this because we generally do not see ourselves as being the roadblock to our success. However, when you tell yourself things like, "I'll do it later", "I just didn't feel like it" and "I'm too tired," in effect, that is what you are doing.

Take The Book, Take The Book

I spoke with a woman recently who is attending school full time. She mentioned that since she had been on spring break, she had not studied at all. She said she "didn't know what it was," but somehow she sat around the house all day and was not motivated to study. I asked her not to feel too bad about it because no matter how sincere we are about completing something, roadblocks will crop up all the time. I suggested that she pick up any one of her books and try walking around the house with it all day. I said no matter where you go and what you do, take the book with you. If you answer the door, take it with you. If you decide to make a peanut butter sandwich, take it with you. Take it everywhere.

The purpose of this exercise was to determine just how long she would deliberately be a hindrance to herself. Anyone who could walk around the house for any length of time with a book in their hands would be compelled to do one of two things. Put the book down, or open it and begin to read it. I am hopeful she did the latter. If you find yourself setting up your own roadblocks, stop and take inventory of the situation. Take some time to write down what has occurred between the time you established the goal and the time you abandoned it. Be honest with yourself. If you find you have been taking naps when you come home from work, write that down. Perhaps you have taken on more than you can handle and feel somewhat overwhelmed. Write that down. You need to document whatever you think you are doing to prevent yourself from being a success. Once you have identified what the obstacle is, put a plan together to overcome that particular restriction. Make certain you do not dwell on it. Just fix it and move on.

Obstacles Imposed By Others

There are other times when you are sincerely and consistently working towards your goal and things happen that thwart your efforts. You could be asked to temporarily work in an area away from where you live. Perhaps there is an ailing child or parent you need to tend to for an extended period of time. You may encounter an envious associate who hampers your efforts. These obstacles are not self-imposed, but they do exist. You don't have to look too far, they just present themselves. Unlike self-imposed obstacles, they appear in more obvious ways, making it easy for us to say "I didn't complete that because . . ." The important point here is not to allow these circumstances to impede your progress. Although they may be obvious roadblocks and you feel there is a good reason why you have not completed the task, you still need to revamp your goals to accommodate changes. Additional obstacles imposed by others could be neighbors who appear at your door just minutes after you come home from work. Funny how they have such perfect timing. It may be someone to whom you have talked about your goals. You cannot seem to understand why this individual continues to come over night after night when he is fully aware of what you have planned for the evenings. Well, it may be difficult for you to understand and believe but this person just may be envious of your ability to follow through on your commitments.

Stand Your Ground And Move On

What you need to do is be firm with your neighbor. Let him know you must get on with your work and that the two of you can talk later. Just imagine what impact that may have on you and your neighbor. For so long, the two of you have spent your evenings together relaxing and sharing the events of the day. Now you have decided to take control of your life. You may have to do this a few more times before your neighbor realizes you are serious about working towards your goals. Having to deal with close friends and relatives in this manner is not easy. But it must be done if you are to complete your goals and be a success.

Probably the most difficult folks you will have to cope with during this process are the ones I refer to as "GoalBusters." These people always look for ways to diminish your dreams. They find fault in almost everything you say you want to do. When you tell them of your goals, they respond in a variety of ways, most of which are negative. They say things like "That's already been done before" or "Boy, that's expensive. You're going to have a tough time getting funding." It does not matter how well thought out your plan is, the GoalBuster will find holes in it, or manufacture them if they are not there. Typically, GoalBusters do not think they are putting you or your goals down. For the most part, they see themselves as being helpful and knowledgeable in all areas. They read a little bit here and there on a particular subject and become an authority overnight. Many will say they know someone who attempted the same thing and was fraught with "one problem after the other." If you know any folks like this, make certain you avoid talking to them about your goals. You should only share your dreams with those individuals who believe in you and are genuinely happy for you. In a subsequent segment, I discuss this in greater detail. If it comes up in a casual conversation and you do not really know this person, respond diplomatically.

You may want to say "You know, that's a good point. I'll think about it. Thanks."

Know that the real joy and excitement of goal setting comes when you stretch your potential and do your best. Aim high and remember your goals need to be big, because it takes a big goal to create the fervor and excitement necessary to attain it.

FIVE
EASY PIECES

It is easy to be popular. It is not easy to be just.

—Rose Bird

I have defined five major elements of a goal that I believe make up its nucleus and are at the foundation of any goal-oriented effort. This nucleus is what I refer to as your goal C.H.A.R.T.© It suggests that your goals are **C**oncise, a **H**abit, **A**ttainable, **R**ealistic and **T**angible. I will describe each one individually.

Concise

Has someone ever given you directions or told you something that wasn't quite clear? I believe this is familiar to everyone. It usually happens as a direct result of one or more of the following:

☐ The individual relaying the information is using too many words to get his point across.

☐ The information is too technical or the individual is using words and slang terminology that makes his delivery confusing and unintelligible.

☐ The person is ambiguous or not saying enough to make his point clear.

Whatever the reason, it all boils down to statements that are unclear, muddled and lengthy. The following is an example of a goal statement:

☐ I will reduce my overall cholesterol consumption by 20 percent.

This statement is straightforward. You know precisely what it is the goal setter wants to accomplish. The statement also tells you to what extent he wants to do this. The goal setter wants to reduce his overall cholesterol consumption by 20 percent. The objectives are:

- ☐ Explore the possibility of preparing recipes low in cholesterol
- ☐ Read labels at the supermarket
- ☐ Look for healthy substitutes
- ☐ Go to restaurants that offer a variety of low cholesterol, healthfully prepared foods and desserts
- ☐ I will begin program 1/1/95

A monthly goal for the cholesterol recipe objective would be to identify the kinds of recipes you want—fish, chicken, pork etc., a weekly goal would be to find three or four recipes by doing some research at the library, reading magazines, newspapers etc. and a daily goal would be to start to document your recipes and become familiar with their benefits.

Since this is an ongoing goal, the process would be repeated until you have accumulated the total number of recipes you determined were necessary to accomplish your goal. Afterwards, a weekly or monthly review and update would suffice. Even a quarterly rolling over or documentation of progress would help keep you motivated and focused. I would be willing to bet you would end up with a full-blown cookbook of your own, customized to suit your taste, appetite and new, healthy lifestyle.

Habit

All great musicians, dancers, athletes and other successful individuals got that way by being consistent. They practiced their skill and made it a part of their lives. These people became totally consumed with the prospect of becoming a success and made each of their talents a habit with them, taking advantage of every opportunity to practice and improve in their area of expertise. Some read about the successes of people in their field of endeavor, learning from their mistakes. Others talked with individuals who succeeded in these areas, and some worked night and day at their craft, stretching their potential until it cried out for mercy, resting only momentarily, then continuing with their efforts. They all share one common denominator, they made their goals a habit.

How do you make your goals a habit? There are a couple of things that contribute to that effort. First, make certain you always document your goals. Remember, you must put pen to paper in order to have a goal. Otherwise, it's just a thought. Make a habit of documenting your goals.

There was a time when I used to trust that I would remember things that crossed my mind throughout the day. I believed that if I just thought about something, I would be able to store it in my memory bank and recall it at will. I soon realized this was not the best way of doing things. After I misplaced a few good thoughts, I began to document them without delay.

Writing things down has become a habit with me. I keep blank paper and a pen on the refrigerator. There's a spiral notebook next to my bed that has sections I've labeled to make recollection easier. I also have a notebook next to the phone, just in case someone phones me and during the course of our conversation, I get the urge to document something that is said or a thought that crosses my mind.

If you are going to be successful at attaining your goals, you must make them a habit. Secondly, your goals need to be in a place where you can view them on a daily basis. I don't mean that you should put them just within view but you need to put place them somewhere you frequent so you can review them regularly.

By dividing your major goal into sub-goals, you challenge yourself daily to accomplish something. For some people, getting through the day is their goal and they muster just enough energy to do that. You know the type; shuffling papers at work, majoring in minors, waving at you each time they pass you in the corridors. Oh, they get through the day all right—to the elevator, their car, through rush hour traffic, past their spouse and children, to the television where they will sit and grunt all evening, until they stumble to bed only to start the same cycle over the next day.

Charlie Cullen once said, "The opportunity for greatness does not come cascading down like a torrential Niagara Falls, but rather it comes slowly, one drop at a time." People, if you want to accomplish your most desired dreams, you simply must work toward your goals each and every day. You must put your plan into practice. Just like the great dancer, musician, athlete and other successful people, you must work at it every day.

Decide right this moment where you want to physically put your goals. Make certain it is a place where you will see them. For some of us, it's an office. Others will put them on the back of their bedroom door. Make your goals a habit and allow them to be a part of your day-to-day activities. If you do this, you will give yourself the emotional and mental perks you need daily, in order to be the success you know you can be.

Attainable

The term attainable should not be used synonymously with realistic. Attaining a goal means you reach or arrive at the set goal; you attained your goal of reducing your overall cholesterol consumption by 20 percent, for example. Thus, you follow through or accomplish the task at hand. To set a realistic goal means that in the process you face facts and see things as factual rather than imaginary. When you set goals, you must be certain you can see them to completion.

Attainable goals do tie in with setting realistic goals; you set yourself up to succeed, and in that regard you accomplish your dreams and desires. At the base of all attainable goals is the belief that you are totally convinced you can reach your target.

This inspiring characteristic allows you to emotionally enjoy the sum total of your goals prior to ever having accomplished them. When this aspect of goal setting is utilized to its fullest potential, it's perhaps the most motivating of all aspects. Attainable goals are akin to the application of self-visualization techniques.

When you use visualization techniques, you relish in the fruition of a goal to the point of being able to almost taste or smell what it will be like once your goal is attained. You may be able to identify with this. Some of you may have recalled an event or song with such clarity that you're able to remember the smell of some food, flower or season of the year when you reminisce. This is the beauty of attainable goals. It keeps you motivated throughout the fulfillment of your desires and sustains you.

Personally, this aspect of goal setting is most effective and motivating for me in terms of how it provides me with the staying power to work through obstacles. When I keep my sight on my goals and take intermittent, mental snapshots of the completion of my dreams and desires, I'm induced to continue. This technique can also be employed to give yourself perks every now and then when you feel a bit drained emotionally.

Visualization is not a new concept; it has been used in a variety of ways. Socrates used to apply this technique during his presentations at Agoura. That was more than twenty-five centuries ago. Self-visualization techniques are mental exercises that constantly remind you of what life will be like tomorrow or the next day.

If you cannot visualize yourself achieving whatever it is you set out to do, chances are you will not apply yourself at the level required to accomplish it. By seeing yourself enjoying the benefits of your goal, you make the transition that much easier and comfortable to enjoy. It is rather difficult to have attainable goals without visualizing them. If you cannot see yourself enjoying your goal—growing, learning and benefitting from it—prior to it ever coming to fruition, you should reassess that particular goal. You may be setting an unrealistic goal and will not be in a position to attain it.

Let me elaborate on this a bit. Many people set goals to please someone else. This could happen for several reasons. You could be trying to please your spouse. You may be experiencing pressures because of family concerns. No matter how much you want to please someone, a goal set for you by someone else will not be sought with as much vim and vigor as a goal you set for yourself. You just will not approach it the same way. If you achieve it, you will have a feeling of accomplishment, but not the same level and intensity as a goal you establish.

Close your eyes now and try to picture yourself talking to someone close to you. This could be a parent, child, spouse, pastor or friend. If you can visualize this scenario, you are on the right path to mastering this concept. Now, see yourself waving goodbye to this person. For those of you who have difficulty doing this, practice this technique throughout the day and look into purchasing books that deal with the mechanics of self-visualization. Afterwards, make it a part of your daily regimen.

Take the very kernel of your deepest desire and goal and see yourself reaping the benefits. Visualize yourself walking away from the podium after receiving a prestigious award, see the beautiful flowers and warm smiling faces of friends and relatives at your wedding. See yourself enjoying the positive interactions with your children. All these things are at the foundation of attainable goals. You see yourself at the finish line, you feel the joy of winning. It has been said that what your mind conceives your heart will achieve. Enjoy the thrill of victory by getting a birds-eye view of your most cherished goals.

Realistic

Another solid characteristic is to make certain your goals are realistic. Most of us believe that if we get jazzed about the idea of losing 70 pounds in three months, we will have the energy, inclination and discipline to do it. However, it is unrealistic to believe you could *safely* gain 70 pounds in three months; so trying to lose it in the same amount of time is not realistic. You must establish realistic goals in order to have a high comfort level with your ability to complete them. Realistic goals are not too far out of reach. They are not beyond your capacity to achieve.

A realistic goal for me, in terms of physical improvement, was to consume a minimum of four glasses of water daily. I started with one in the morning, another after lunch, one glass after dinner and the last glass one hour before bed. I believed this goal to be something within my reach and realistic. Not since I was a child had I drunk so much water on a daily basis. As a child, I drank tons of water because I played outside a lot with my friends and got really thirsty. This type of activity warrants the consumption of plenty of water. Today, I continue to follow this daily regimen, altering it upwards. Usually, I keep a large pitcher on my desk filled with water.

Do not conclude that just because someone says you will not be able to achieve your goal that it is unrealistic. It could be that the individual you have chosen to share this information with is not genuinely happy about your desires or successes. Wisdom tells us that we should not share our plans and desires too promiscuously. I will devote an entire chapter to the ill-effects of sharing your goals with others, but for now, understand that setting unrealistic goals causes anxieties. When you set any goal that is out of your reach, you do yourself a disfavor. Because the goal is unrealistic, you are setting yourself up to lose. When trying to determine whether or not your goal is realistic, ask yourself these questions:

- ☐ Is my goal too far into the future?
- ☐ Am I involving luck as a barometer for success?
- ☐ Is this a goal set for me by someone else?
- ☐ Is my goal unreasonably big?

How to Develop **A GOAL MIND** ....

Look at each of these individually. If your goal is too far into the future, you won't have a target close enough to hit. In addition, you may lose sight of your goal and abandon it altogether. Goals set too far into the future are goals that are out of sight (in a bad sense). We have all heard the saying, out of sight, out of mind. This is true for your goals as well. If it is too far off, you cannot embrace it and may become disenchanted. Most often, we end up putting those goals on the proverbial back burner.

When you involve luck, you are on a sure path of despair and disillusionment. People who win in life use their own talents and keep them constantly honed. These folks don't look for the big break or the get-rich-quick schemes. They know their big break comes with commitment and sheer determination. As I mentioned earlier, if you are working towards a goal that is set by someone else, you certainly will not approach it with the energy and commitment you would for a goal you set for yourself.

Finally, goals that are unrealistically big are unmanageable. If it is too big and you miss it by a lot, it may have a negative impact towards subsequent goals. Sometimes, people set really big goals purposely so they can have a host of excuses for their deficiencies. These same individuals look to friends and relatives to be understanding of their failures. They don't expect them to be judgmental. Quite often they are not, because they want you to succeed. So remember, it is imperative that your goals be realistic. By doing this, you set yourself up for success; you feel good about what it is you are attempting to do and your ability to pull it off.

Tangible

You define the essence of your desires by stating a tangible goal. This particular aspect lends a lot of credence to your goal statements. It provides meaning and significance to your objectives for each goal. The first thing that comes to mind when I think about tangible goals is that they must have substance. I liken this characteristic to something I can feel. By adding substance to your goals, in effect, you add relevance.

Tangible goals help you define the reasons why you are establishing a particular goal. In other words, when you set a goal, you not only need to know what it is you are striving for but why. That is the reason this element is so important, because it describes your intentions and beliefs. When you ask an individual why they have set a particular goal, you should hear some of the following statements:

- ☐ I want to do this because I have great organizational skills
- ☐ I enjoy motivating others
- ☐ This is a natural talent for me
- ☐ I have excellent interpersonal skills

All of these reasons have substance and define the general fabric of the goal. There will be times, however, when you ask someone why they established a certain goal and you may hear some of the following responses:

- ☐ Oh, I don't know, it seems interesting
- ☐ That profession pays well
- ☐ It seems everyone is doing it. Don't you agree?

If the person begins to hem and haw and say these things, you will know right away they have not given much thought to the goal and it is not a tangible goal for them. If you cannot substantiate the reason for wanting to accomplish a goal, it may not be right for you. And remember, it must have relevance and importance and you must have faith in your ability to achieve it.

The five C.H.A.R.T.© elements will assist you in accomplishing your most valued dreams. For each goal statement, make certain you are able to apply each of these components in order to obtain maximum results. If you need to alter your objectives, do so with confidence, knowing that you have a firm foundation to establish your goals.

TAKE TIME
To make timE

If a close friend phoned and offered you a two week trip for two to the Bahamas, if you left in three days, would you take it? Initially, you would be jubilant at the prospect of getting away for two weeks. You may have to stop and think about how you could get away on such short notice. You would probably discuss it with your significant other and decide it is well worth it to put everything aside for a while and enjoy some sun and fun. Later, you would phone your friend, accept the offer and afterwards, enumerate all the things you needed to do in order to prepare for the trip.

My question to you would be, if you could shore up this much energy to organize yourself to take a trip, why not mentally prepare yourself to go to the Bahamas every day? How can you do this? By planning a perfect day, every day. The first thing you need to do is make certain you organize your time into several segments each day. How you decide to segment each day is up to you and based on what kind of individual you are. You will attempt the same task given to a thousand different people in your own unique way.

Developing A Personal Goal

Some time ago, I set a goal for myself to read one book a month. It has been working quite well. I never had a problem reading periodicals, newsletters and a variety of magazine articles and would occasionally read a "how to" book. However, when it came to reading a novel, I found myself reading a total of six or seven chapters in my spare time, but never finishing. I would have bookmarks in several books, but none ever read in its entirety. In order to accomplish this goal, I began bringing books with me everywhere I went. During a fifteen-minute break or lunch hour, I would take that opportunity to read. I reached a point where I did this every day, unless I had an errand to run. In no time, I would complete a book and start another one. Now that I have a small child, that has not stopped me. I read while he takes a bath or naps. When I'm in the waiting room at the doctor's office, I read. I even take a book to the park and anywhere I would normally have some inactive time. My point is this; take the time to identify what is best for you. Let your individuality shine. Do what works for you. Put a plan together and by all means stick to it. Once you put a plan in motion and consistently carry it through, you'll find it becomes effortless and you're motivated to do even more. But don't let a day go by without doing *something*. Too much idle time leads to mental malnutrition and puts a damper on your perfect day.

Seize The Moment

Have you ever wished to relive a day or incident just so you would be able to handle it differently? For some of us, it was because we wasted time doing something insignificant when we could have spent the time improving upon our lot, enriching our minds and exposing ourselves to a something new. You must be willing to put your time and energy into improving areas of your life that require immediate attention and less time on those items of least importance. Never make excuses and always remember, take time to make time. If you do not seize the moment and you are wanting success, then you are a dreamer. Many dreamers have money-making, thought-provoking ideas. The only problem is they are just dreams. They wake up in the morning, jump into the shower and begin dreaming about the big plans they will put into action. The only problem is, they never get out of the shower.

I challenge each of them to spend twenty minutes documenting what they do on any given evening at home. Be brutally honest. If you plan on going home to do some gardening but find yourself interrupted by a phone call, write down how much time you spent doing that. There is a certain amount of time spent recovering from these interruptions and it really takes its toll on our time.

How Much Time Do You Waste?

On any given evening, assuming you spend your days working a nine to five job, you will find that you spend about three and-a-half hours of idle time. For some, that figure is doubled on Saturdays and Sundays. That amounts to about one day a week. *Unbelievable!!!* Just take a look at the number of successful people in the world. You will not have to look very hard to see that there are more poor and needy than wealthy. Besides financial wealth, what do these individuals have that you do not have or that you want? They eat, sleep, eat, drink and think. Yet they have accumulated great wealth and status and many continue to relish the fruits of their labor. What is the difference? Actually, it is quite simple. They have a burning desire to be more than they are today and half as much as they will be tomorrow. As a matter of fact, they do not ever see themselves failing at anything. They know when they set a goal, no matter what obstacles confront them or what level of accomplishment they achieve, they are a success because they've accepted the challenge.

These folks have a propensity towards greatness and goodness. When you come in contact with an individual of this nature, you will either be put off or inspired. If you are put off, it may be because you see the person as forcing the behavior or attitude. However, this behavior can be learned to the point that it becomes a part of your natural enthusiasm. Do not squander your days away when you can use them to work towards the good that is yours in your divine right. You owe it to yourself to look at ways you can extract the most from each day. Do this and you will achieve all of your dreams.

CHAPTER FOURTEEN

YOU REAP
WHAT YOU SOW

Oh, what a
tangled web we
weave, when first
we practice to
deceive.

—Sir Walter Scott

If you remember that growth is nature's first law, you will realize that whatever is planted or started must grow. Just think back on a grade school project when everyone planted a few seeds in a used milk carton. Your teacher would have each student print his or her name on the outside of the carton and place it on the ledge of the classroom window. As each day passed, everyone would watch eagerly as their seeds developed into strong green plants. The transformation process created excitement from you and the other students.

Perhaps no other activity demonstrates the positive effects reaping and sowing has on our psyche as well as this one. We generally do not relate the process of reaping and sowing to our thoughts. But our thoughts have a lot to do with how weak or strong, successful or unsuccessful we are. It is important to understand the impact our thoughts have on our subconscious mind. The subconscious mind is involuntary and quite instinctive. It never sleeps, it creates our dreams and can't distinguish between what is real or fiction. These thoughts can sometimes turn negative and we recover feeling disturbed, troubled and emotionally drained. Because you have allowed your thoughts to get away with you, your subconscious takes over and without separating fact from fantasy, it vicariously permits you to live the thoughts you impress upon it. In each scenario, essentially, you are reaping the essence of your thoughts.

A Natural High

Doctors agree that whenever we are happy, the body releases chemicals called endorphins. When secreted from the brain, they have a comforting influence on our mind and physical state. In a recent test of this theory, individuals were asked to act out scenes from a play. Some were asked to read doleful, sad scenes while others read uplifting and stimulating scenes. All were asked to read with much expression. The endorphin levels of the individuals who read the sad passages dropped and were virtually non-existent, while those who read the stimulating scenes released very high levels of endorphins.

We can all remember being very angry at someone or even having an altercation or argument. In thinking about these situations, did you ever notice how long it takes you to recover emotionally from these negative situations? It is frightening how long it takes. I can tell you from experience, it takes a lot of negative energy, too. Let us explore another aspect of negative energy. It is called gossip or hearsay. We have all heard the expression, "what goes around, comes around." Well, the same is true for negative talk. When we spread rumors about someone, we are putting ourselves in a position to receive the same.

An Expensive Lesson

Early in my professional career, I learned a lesson regarding gossip. There were many opportunities for me to rub elbows with some of the most influential people in the company. One day, the vice president of our division was visiting a few of the department managers. After her visit, she was on her way towards the elevators and stopped to ask me how things were going. I began to enumerate all the wonderful and exciting things my area was involved in and casually mentioned something I had heard with respect to another individual's "tenuous" position with the company. Later, my manager brought it to my attention. I can tell you, I never felt so foolish and ashamed about gossiping as I did that day. I truly mean it when I say whatever you say and think will come back to you.

If You Can't Say Something Nice ...

Have you ever gossiped about someone and later discovered that others were discussing you in an uncomplimentary way? What goes around comes around. There is not one person who can honestly say they have not told someone something in confidence that didn't get back to others for whom the story was not intended. We seriously need to understand the impact of our words and thoughts. If you think injurious thoughts about someone it is for sure someone, will do the same towards you.

If this is difficult to put this into practice, take a step-by-step approach. Just tell yourself you are feasting on cerebral junk food and that you need to adjust your behavior. Any time I want to adjust my behavior and it requires unwavering determination, I always begin with my family. Besides, your family is inclined to be more honest with you. Knowing that you have a somewhat discriminating audience, you can immediately get to work. Never feel that you are handicapped by conditions, because conditions are simply the result of some previous shortage of something else. You can and will modify any unwanted conduct.

Reaping what you sow is a dominant and significant aspect in the game of life. You can rest assured that the thoughts you throw out into the universe unquestionably come back to you. Always remember that they never come back the way you render them. Although you can expect a harvest, the crop may be contaminated by the tainted seeds you planted when you gossiped, entertained bad thoughts about another, or pondered bad deeds towards someone. A good rule of thumb is: it is always best to believe the purposes and intentions of others. Your view towards others is an indication of your own inner condition. To the blameless all things are pure. Altering your behavior to this method of belief will keep you so full of sound and healthy thoughts you will have no time for idle chatter. Robust and vigorous thoughts will facilitate your getting rid of what Zig Ziglar calls stinkin' thinkin. You will look better, feel better and spread an attitude that's infectious.

CHAPTER FIFTEEN

TALK IS
NOT CHEAP

*Although the
tongue weighs
very little,
few people are
able to hold it.*

—Anonymous

It is often true that people believe they can force the attainment of their desires just by talking about them. If this is your belief, consider the correlation between the usefulness of talk compared to the effectiveness of thought or meditation. It has been said that a person's life is influenced 10 percent by his conscious mind and 90 percent by his subconscious mind. This being the case, we could say everyday conversation is directly responsible for a mere 10 percent of the good that befalls us. Even if everything you said was 100 percent positive, it would only account for 10 percent of the good you encounter on a daily basis. Therefore, it is essential for you to exercise every possible option that provides you an opportunity to maximize your conscious thinking. The things you desire most are the things you need to talk about least. Initally, this concept may be one that is challenging for you to grasp and set in motion. Once you make the decision to start and begin to employ this technique, you will find it quite valuable. Your biggest challenge may be your ability to consistently hold your tongue when sharing some of your most cherished dreams. It is difficult to avoid telling friends and relatives the progress you are making on your goals. I am not saying you should not share your goals with immediate family members. However, it does no one any good if you talk about them in excess. There is no value added to the process at all. Especially if you have a tendency to embellish the truth. Elaborating leads to a let down feeling later, when you have time to reflect on the things. You may ask yourself why you fabricated the truth. No matter how you try to justify your statements, if you have any sense of conscience you will feel bad. Hopefully, you will not make a habit of this behavior and end up abandoning your goals because of it. I stated in an earlier segment that seeds dug up and inspected do not grow to their full potential. Talking excessively about things you want to do is equivalent to putting your goals under constant verbal scrutiny. In other words, talking about them incessantly puts them under a microscope for you and everyone else to examine. Thus, they do not take the shape and ultimate form you intended for them. The growth is stunted and you cannot say with confidence that the goal was fully attained.

I Know Somebody Like That

I used to work with a woman who always seemed to be able to identify with whatever anyone was saying. If someone was having a bad day, she would tell you she had come in contact with someone that morning who had also gotten off to a bad start—never mentioning names, just knowing someone. When her manager shared the loss of a loved one, she knew someone who experienced the same type of loss. She talked excessively. When she was not engaged in dialogue with anyone, she talked to herself. You could hear her over the cubicles, asking herself questions and answering herself. It seemed no matter what she did, she announced it. Whether it was going to get a drink of water, going to a meeting or to lunch. She would say things like: "Well, I better go to lunch," or "I need a drink of water," and "I've got a quick meeting to attend." In addition to all this pointless talk, she would tell anyone who would listen that her children hardly ever wanted to visit her. Her idle talk prevented her from enjoying life's simple pleasures and kept most people and family members at a distance. She did not understand the true meaning of the American Indian proverb: Listen or thy tongue will keep thee deaf. Believe me when I say no one accomplishes much by insignificant talk. Instead of talking a great deal about your dreams and goals, you should spend a lot of time impressing these thoughts on your subconscious mind. This approach will serve you well as you go about your daily chores and even as you sleep because your subconscious mind remains active. Remember, it never sleeps.

Just Keep It To Yourself

Not long ago, I was on my way to lunch with a friend. We ran into a mutual acquaintance who used to work in our office. We stopped to chat for a while and in talking, asked what brought him to our company. Our friend simply replied, "I have a meeting." My lunch partner asked, "Oh, who are you meeting?" Our friend answered "I'd rather not say at this time." As my co-worker and I approached his car he responded, "Boy, he was really tight-lipped about that." I indicated that I felt he was wise not to mention that information. By doing so, he would have given us an implied consent to mention it to others. Secondly, he would lessen his potential for success. If he had discussed it with us, he might somehow believe he confirmed its positive outcome. Lastly, sharing it with us may make him feel uneasy about it later. So in every way imaginable, this was a wise decision for him to keep it to himself.

Think, Then Act

Ponder your dreams and ambitions and make certain you create as many sincere affirmations about them as you can. If it just so happens that you resolve to share your dreams with someone, it should be someone who shares the same desires and goals. It should be a person who is genuinely happy for you and not negative of your plans. In addition to sharing your plans, you should never talk about them for the sake of self-importance. Death and life are in the power of the tongue. When I am tempted to share something too freely with someone, I quickly remind myself of this.

Whenever I am enticed to speak on a subject that is near and dear to my heart, I listen to the gentle, yet strong voice within. Have you experienced flashes of intuition that proved true when you kept them to yourself? I can recall talking with people who have stopped in the middle of what they were saying and paused or put their hand to their mouth. I quietly acknowledge the gesture, because I understand and respect their ability to hold their tongue at appropriate times. No one needs to talk in insignificant detail about the things they plan to do. Dale Carnegie said, "You can make more friends in two months by becoming interested in other people than you can in two years by trying to get other people interested in you." If you allow others to talk, you learn, there is less chance for you to say something you may later regret having shared, and you will make friends, to boot.

For those of you who C.H.A.R.T.© a course of action for your life, do not talk about it much. Think about it and meditate on it. In this way, you will release the full potential and power of your subconscious mind. Meditate on your aspirations so that your subconscious mind will be strengthened to help you as you work through your goals.

YOUR CUP
Runneth oveR

They shall still bring forth fruit in old age; they shall be fat and flourishing.

—Psalm 92:14

Surely, goodness and mercy shall follow me all the days of my life...." I get goose bumps whenever I hear or read these words from the 23rd Psalm. I am certain that my needs are being met continuously and that I am prospering in all areas of my life. So, prosperity is what I want to communicate in this segment. Think about all the resources available to us that contribute to our success. We have migrated from an agricultural society to an industrial society and now have become an information society. We have at our fingertips a flood of information from a variety of sources: satellite, microwave and computers, with which to gain insight and expand our perspective on any topic. We now have access to more information in one day than our grandparents were exposed to in their entire lifetimes. There is no reason why anyone should be without a resource to help them solve or work through any issue that confronts them. There is a slogan our local phone company uses to market their yellow pages directory. They say, "If you can't find it here, maybe it doesn't exist." The same is true for the multitude of resources we have available. If you cannot find it, perhaps it does not exist and you just created an opportunity for yourself to try to develop it. Recently, a woman told me she had to pull together a business proposal. She asked if I had anything she could review because she "couldn't find any information on how to complete a proposal." I asked who was requesting the proposal and whether or not they provided her with any input as to the topics they wanted included. She said, "Well, my manager is requesting it and I told her I knew how to put it together." I gave her some feedback on how she should structure it and told her I did not have anything I could share with her by her due date (three days from the day of our conversation). I also suggested she go to the library. Here is an example of someone not tapping into the vast amount of resources available to everyone.

Find The Good In You

Just for a moment, reflect on the natural talents you have. Do not cut yourself short. Think about all the things you enjoy doing and that are second nature to you. Is it cooking, organizing, acting? We sometimes have a tendency to overlook our own talents and make comments such as, "I don't really have any talents per se." Or we may mention the fact that we are "nowhere near the abilities of Mary Jane or Bill." This self-defeating attitude could wreak havoc on your potential for success. It is no wonder we do not get the good that is part of our divine inheritance. You must never belittle your abilities. If it is wrong to ridicule the acts of another person, then the same is true for you. Can you recall a time when you built up the self-esteem of another and how it helped them reach their dream? Well, you can also build that same faith in your abilities by refusing to downplay them to yourself or others. With this understanding, you will never resort to such statements as "I am lacking" or "I could never do that." To subscribe to those affirmations is tantamount to denying that you have any natural talents. Those of you who use the technique to your advantage receive a bountiful harvest.

Don't Worry, Be Happy

We spend an inordinate amount of time worrying. It has a lot to do with two of the most common obstacles preventing us from maximizing our potential—fear and worry. We fear failure, defeat and loss. When you direct more energy into worry thoughts, you channel less energy into good thoughts. Fear, doubt and worry are nothing more than a lack of faith and good thoughts. They have no more power than you give them. Without your input, they would not exist. There is no reason why we all cannot be prosperous. In order to build prosperity, many folks believe they have to deal with two separate forces, good and bad. That is not true. If you were cold, you would simply build a fire or turn on the heat and the cold would dissipate. Prosperity is one side of a two-sided coin. Once you realize this, it is easier to achieve your goals. An old Hindustan proverb says, "The crow, whilst learning to walk like a swan, forgot its own gait." You can attract more prosperity if you are not inclined to worry over some apparent obstacle. When you find yourself worrying over foolish things, remind yourself of the illusions of the physical senses. Because our mind does not know the difference between fact and fiction, you can feed it the things you want and revamp any situation to your benefit. Alter your mode of living to not see two powers, good and evil, right and wrong. See that there is but one power, good, and it is the only law of life. If you have not found this power, it is not necessarily because you have not taken the right approach. It may be that you have not looked far enough for this one principle that is the basis of all life. Your physical and human power is nothing in comparison to the full power of this principle. Have you ever thought about your possessions and how they came to you? Everything you possess has come to you because you have given its equivalent in some form. Perhaps you have provided for someone's needs by giving food, shelter, prayer or money. Let your giving be in a manner that brings you the things you want.

Give, Give, Give, Then Give Some More

Many people have given to humankind in one way or another. One individual was John D. Rockefeller. It has been estimated that he gave away more than half a billion dollars. He was more than aware of the importance of giving and receiving. He gave when he had little to give. If we further probe this law further and its relationship to prosperity, it appears that the law is a two-way one. We may believe that in order to benefit from this law, we need to balance the giving and receiving. However, all we need to do is take care of the giving and the receiving will take care of itself. As a matter of fact, the less emphasis we place on the receiving side of this law the better. You may pass prosperity on to another in many forms. As I mentioned earlier, it may be in the form of food, shelter or prayer. But do not make the mistake of thinking that you can fool this divine law of giving and receiving. One of the greatest hindrances in people's lives is that they dwell too much on receiving something and trying to force things to manifest themselves. If this is true, why is it that some people get things without asking while others beg and do not receive anything? The reason for this is the one who receives has set his mind on giving. The person who sets his mind on receiving has put all his thoughts on begging and is forcing the situation.

If It Don't Fit, Don't Force It

When you get the urge to try to force good things to come to you, remember how much more you will enjoy that good when it comes to you naturally. Force is an instrument of destructive processes. Constantly remind yourself of the law of prosperity. It is giving and receiving. Know that when you give freely, you increase prosperity tenfold. The spiritual law says that the resulting good will take a natural course and will give the greatest supply to the greatest number, multiply itself and make its way back to the giver. In order to apply the principles of goal setting defined in this book, you must also apply the laws of prosperity. As mentioned before, look at the goal and make certain you have divided it into several manageable pieces. If you get off the track, revamp your objectives and continue. Never, ever, ever give in to defeat and remind yourself that determination and self-confidence gets you through every situation.

As you continue to establish your goals and learn how to effectively use the left and right brain, there is no way for you to go but up. After consistent efforts, one day you will realize the traits have been there all along; you just did not exercise your rights to apply them. Perhaps, you did not have a plan, but you do now.

Learn to make the most of your time and eliminate the time busters and GoalBusters. As always, remember to write things down and do not trust or believe you will be able to recall them at will. This just will not happen. As you accomplish a goal, make sure to reward yourself. It will not hurt to have a "buddy system" in place, someone like yourself who wants to seriously improve themselves. Share your dreams with this individual, help keep them motivated, and ask that they do the same for you. Remember, if the heart believes, the mind can achieve. Keep your thoughts fresh, spiritual and motivating. Do not allow the presence of fear and try to avoid folks who have nothing good or pleasant to share with you.

The fact that you read this book demonstrates your sincere desire to work at improving yourself. Keep this book in a place where you can access it quickly and make certain you refer to it often. Best wishes, and God bless you in all your efforts.

Index